HINDUISM
AND ITS
RELATIONS TO CHRISTIANITY

HINDUISM

AND ITS

RELATIONS TO CHRISTIANITY

JOHN ROBSON, M. A.

GYAN

Published by

Gyan Publishing House
5, Ansari Road
Daryaganj, New Delhi-110002
Phone: 011-47034999, 9811692060
E-mail: books@gyanbooks.com

Distribution Network
gyanbooks.com
India, USA, Canada, UK, Australia, France

ISBN: 978-81-212-8706-7 (PB)
First Published, 1874

2nd Impression 2023

Printed at: Gyan Press, Delhi.

HINDUISM AND ITS RELATIONS TO CHRISTIANITY
Author: John Robson

HINDUISM

AND ITS

RELATIONS TO CHRISTIANITY

BY THE

REV. JOHN ROBSON, M.A.

FORMERLY OF AJMER.

EDINBURGH: WILLIAM OLIPHANT & CO.

GLASGOW: DAVID ROBERTSON.

LONDON: HAMILTON, ADAMS & CO.

1874

TO THE

Rev. John Wilson, D.D., F.R.S.

OF THE FREE CHURCH MISSION, BOMBAY,

WHO, DURING FORTY-FIVE YEARS, WHILE SEEKING FAITHFULLY

TO COMMEND TO THE HINDUS THE TRUTH OF CHRISTIANITY,

HAS SHOWN HIMSELF A DILIGENT AND APPRECIATIVE

STUDENT OF THEIR LITERATURE AND RELIGION,

This Book is Dedicated

AS A MARK OF AFFECTION AND ESTEEM.

PREFACE.

THIS book is offered to those who take an interest in India, and especially in Indian missions, as an attempt to enable them better to understand the religion of the great majority of the people of that land. I have found prevalent in this country ideas of Hinduism very different from those which a twelve years' practical study of it in constant contact with its followers has led me to form. Generally, among friends of missions, there is an undue depreciation of Hinduism,—an ignoring or an ignorance of the amount of truth and vitality still to be found in it; whilst, among those indifferent or hostile to missions, there is an equal ignoring or ignorance of the falsehood which vitiates that truth and poisons that vitality. Not only does Hinduism contain a subtle philosophy, express high moral truths and enjoin many social virtues; it even in one guise or other embodies many of the leading religious truths which Christianity teaches. But that there is in it an ineradicable vice which neutralizes all that is good, which has paralyzed and must paralyze all those efforts at reform within Hinduism that more enlightened Hindus have made and are now making, and which leaves Christianity the only hope for India—is what I have endeavoured to show.

The present religion of India can be better understood with some knowledge of those faiths which preceded it. I have therefore prefixed a short sketch of the earlier religions of India, for which I have availed myself of the results of the investigations of others, principally Max Müller's *Early Sanskrit Literature*, and *Science of Religion*; Professor H. H. Wilson's *Translation of the Rig Veda*; Dr. John Wilson's *India Three Thousand Years Ago*; Lassen's *Indische Alterthumskunde*; and that thesaurus of Indian literature, *Sanskrit Texts*, by Dr. John Muir, to whose hints and assistance I am otherwise indebted. The remainder of the book is mainly the result of my own observations and study of the sacred literature now most current among the Hindus. But, being unable to procure in this country many of the books I wished, I have been obliged to depend greatly on memory, and to leave out many particular references which I could have desired to give.

Since this volume was sent to the press I have read the third volume of Talboys Wheeler's *History of India*.[1] I was glad to find that many of my positions were confirmed by his investigations, though, as was perhaps inevitable in a field so vast and still so uncertain, many of our conclusions are quite different. I have been able, in the latter chapters on Hinduism and in the Appendix, to introduce some notes from his work where it bears on the question in hand.

A discussion has lately appeared in the pages of the *Fortnightly Review* between Mr. Lyall and Max Müller on the missionary character and vitality of the Brahmanical religion. It has evidently in a great measure sprung from a misconception of the meaning of the latter in his lecture on Missions in Westminster Abbey, and might not have been raised

[1] This third volume, published by Trübner and Co., is complete in itself, and—while not presenting the same complete chronicle of events which other histories do—presents a far more interesting and vivid picture of what is characteristic and permanent in India, of the inner life and social condition of the people, of all that it is important for us to know about them, than any other history with which I am acquainted. The first and second volumes, dealing rather with Indian histories, do for Sanskrit literature what the 'Greek and Latin Classics for English Readers' have done for Greek and Latin literature, and enable the English reader pleasantly and profitably to become acquainted with the voluminous historical poems of the Hindus.

had Mr. Lyall seen the Lecture in its published form instead of the report in the *Times.* This, however, is hardly to be regretted, as it has led to the appearance of Mr. Lyall's vivid account of Brahmanical propagandism, which will, I believe, be vouched for as true in its main features [2] by those who have had to do with Brahmanism, where it has been less affected by European enlightenment. It is perhaps unfortunate that the term Brahmanism should be used, for in its strict sense it means merely the religion of the Brahmans, and is utterly non-expansive. It can be professed only by them, and no one can be a Brahman who is not born one. But if we take that system which places the Brahmans at the head, but includes also the religion of the

2 Mr. Lyall seems to me to speak somewhat unguardedly as to the miraculous agency employed by the Brahmans. They pretend to have the power to bring the god into the image by the use of charms, but I never met or heard of a Brahman who pretended to have the power of working miracles, as we understand them, or who applied to any one who pretended to have it any other name than *Pàkhand*—cheat. In the earlier years of the Rajputana Mission, several persons pretended to be inspired by the goddess Màtà, and to have the power of working miracles, but they were all ignorant and illiterate members of low castes. Dr. Valentine, then medical missionary at Beawr, on one occasion gave one of them, when he pretended to be inspired, some *liquor ammoniæ* to smell, which so stunned and confounded him, that he confessed himself a cheat. Since then the miracle-mongers have kept out of reach of the *padre's* medicine-bottle.

Rajputs, the religion of the Baniyas, and of every caste that may come within its pale, and which may more appropriately be termed Hinduism, then it is expansive, though it is proselytizing rather than missionary; and it proselytizes by absorbing tribes, not by converting individuals.

But Hinduism has still great vitality. Max Müller, after describing in his Lecture the most popular gods of the Hindu pantheon, adds: 'But ask any Hindu who can read and write and think, whether these are the gods he believes in, and he will smile at your credulity.' And in his article he says, 'I ask Mr. Lyall, is this true or is it not?' If he will allow me to answer this question, I would say that perhaps a definition of the word 'think' might remove misconception, but, in so far as I understand his words, and in so far as my experience goes, I would say 'it is not true.' I have met Hindus who could read and write and think, and who soberly, firmly, and acutely maintained their faith in Vishnu and Siva, and even in the efficacy of worshipping their images. And if he has any difficulty in conceiving how it should be so, I would relate a rencontre, to which I was witness, between a Christian Brahman, who had visited this country, and an American.

'I am very much surprised,' said the American, 'that any of a race so intelligent as yours should be idolaters.'

'I am very much surprised,' replied the Brahman, 'that any of a race so intelligent as yours should be idolaters. I came to England by Rome, and I saw English and Americans kissing the toe of Jupiter, said to be St. Peter, and worshipping images just as much as the Hindus do.'

I do not write this because I take any despairing view of the future of Christianity in India, but because, as Mr. Lyall puts it, 'those who go to war there must, for many a long day, take Brahmanism into their strategic account.' In writing this book I had the hope and prospect of returning to bear my part personally in this great war. Though I have been obliged meanwhile to relinquish this hope, neither my interest in the work of evangelizing India, nor my confidence in its ultimate triumph, is at all abated; and if this book should succeed at all in strengthening these sentiments in Christians in this country, I shall consider myself amply rewarded for any labour I may have expended on it.

LANGSIDE, GLASGOW, *September* 1874.

CONTENTS.

INTRODUCTION.

PART I.

EARLIER RELIGIONS OF INDIA.

PART II.

HINDUISM.

PART III.

HINDUISM AND MAHOMMEDANISM.

PART IV.

HINDUISM AND CHRISTIANITY.

APPENDIX.

ERRATA.

Page 13, line 21, *for* glimpses *read* glimpse.
,, 101, ,, 3, ,, equipose ,, equipoise.
,, 137, ,, 23, ,, evidenly ,, evidently.
,, 302, ,, 3, ,, , ,, .
,, 81, Note 5, delete (50).

'History seems to teach that the whole human race required a gradual education before, in the fulness of time, it could be admitted to the truths of Christianity. All the fallacies of human reason had to be exhausted before the light of a higher truth could meet with ready acceptance. The ancient religions of the world were but the milk of nature, which was in due time to be succeeded by the bread of life. After the primeval physiolatry, which was common to all the members of the Aryan family, had, in the hands of a wily priesthood, been changed into an empty idolatry, the Indian alone, of all the Aryan nations, produced a new form of religion, which has well been called subjective, as opposed to the more objective worship of nature. That religion, the religion of Buddha, has spread far beyond the limits of the Aryan world, and, to our limited vision, it may seem to have retarded the advent of Christianity among a large portion of the human race. But in the sight of Him with whom a thousand years are but as one day, that religion, like all the ancient religions of the world, may have but served to prepare the way of Christ, by helping through its very errors to strengthen and to deepen the ineradicable yearning of the human heart after the truth of God.'—MAX MULLER, *Ancient Sanskrit Literature.*

INTRODUCTION.

AN Englishman, entering for the first time a native town in India, will probably not proceed far without having his attention drawn to an open shrine, containing a rudely carved stone, worshipped with rites as senseless as their object is shapeless. Let him ask one of the worshippers a 'reason of the faith that is in him,' and he will as probably be taken aback with a subtle reply, revealing a system of thought entirely distinct from his, depending on other bases and proceeding by other methods, and the fallacy of which he cannot at the moment seize. Further experience will show him that the reply he has received is a stock reply, the fruit of the thinking of the nation rather than of the individual; but the first impression produced will be one of bewilderment, perplexing his reason, and throwing him back on his instincts for evidence of the truth.

A similar bewilderment, I fancy, must be produced on many when they read accounts of the religion of the Hindus by persons who have had opportunities of observing it from different points of view. Some speak of it as the grossest of superstitions; others, as the deepest and subtlest of speculations. Macaulay, who had to do with the Hindus as a legislator, can hardly find words strong enough to denounce their faith. 'In no part of the world,' he says, 'has a religion ever existed more unfavourable to the moral and intellectual health of our race. The Brahmanical mythology is so absurd that it necessarily debases every mind which receives it as truth. And with this absurd mythology is bound up an absurd system of physics, an absurd geography, an absurd astronomy. Nor is this form of Paganism more favourable to art than to religion. Through the whole of the Hindu Pantheon you will look in vain for anything resembling those beautiful and majestic forms which stood in the shrines of ancient Greece. All is hideous and grotesque and ignoble. As

Macaulay's opinion of Hinduism.

this superstition is of all superstitions the most irrational and of all superstitions the most inelegant, so is it of all superstitions the most immoral. Emblems of vice are objects of public worship. Acts of vice are acts of public worship. The courtesans are as much a part of the establishment of the temple, as much ministers of the god as the priests. Crimes against life, crimes against property, are not only permitted but enjoined by this odious theology. But for our interference human victims would still be offered to the Ganges, and the widow would still be laid on the pile by the corpse of her husband, and be burned alive by her own children.'[1]

Ballantyne's opinion.

Compare this testimony with that of another, who had to deal with the Hindus as a scholar and a philosopher, and who declares Hindu philosophy to be 'a calm, clear, collected exposition of principles, which Germany constantly and England occasionally gropes after, without ever grasping them with any such grasp as that with which India

[1] Speech on the Gates of Somnauth.

has taken hold on them.'[2] This is the language not of an opponent of Christianity but of an advocate, taken from a book designed to lead Hindu pundits to a careful study of its truths. It is moreover on the whole a fair statement of the case. Hindu philosophers live in a world of thought such as Europeans can form little idea of. The practical and real questions that are ever present to the mind of the German, and still more of the Englishman, leading them to tread with doubt and hesitation, if not with humility, never trouble the Hindu metaphysician at all. He moves in the region of pure thought, unimpeded by the contradictions which retard the course of his Western brethren, on to the goal of a transcendental abstraction from which the most daring of them would shrink.

Characteristics of Hindu philosophy.

Practical application of Hindu philosophy.

But man is not all thought; he has an outward life which he must lead, actual relations which he must fulfil, yearnings and aspirations of the soul which he must satisfy. The real value of a system is found when it

[2] Ballantyne's *Bible for the Pundits.*

comes to deal practically with these questions, and the practical result of Hindu philosophy in dealing with them is that hideous picture which Macaulay has drawn, not one trait of which is too dark, but of which he saw only the outer form without noting the subtle soul of Pantheism that pervades it, justifying its grossest excesses and wildest extravagances. It is this union of a subtle Pantheistic philosophy with a gross popular idolatry that constitutes modern Hinduism, and makes it the most redoubtable foe with which Christianity has to contend in India if not in the world.

History of Hinduism.

Looking at this system as it now exists, examining the books that are current among the people, conversing with them and debating with their teachers, we can form some idea of the bases of thought on which it now rests and of the hold which it has on the Hindu mind. But the question irresistibly occurs, How did men come to believe in such a system? Can there possibly be any kinship between it and the faith which we profess? Are there common principles in our nature to which both alike appeal? Hinduism as it now is was not always the religion of India, and indeed in its present form it is of comparatively modern date. Just as in looking at the rocks of the Jura or the red sandstone of Cromarty, and studying the fossils imbedded therein, we feel sure that we are looking on the vestiges of a former world; so in studying modern Hinduism, we feel that we have the fossilized remains of former faiths, gathered into new combinations and welded together by a new power. But as to the real history of the changes that have taken place, we are still comparatively in the dark. The student of Hinduism has indeed more to guide him than the student of Geology, but after all that has been done much is still uncertain, much is left to conjecture.

Yet the main features of the past religious history of India have been determined with sufficient accuracy for practical purposes, and modern Hinduism can be best understood by looking first of all at those religions which preceded it. I will, therefore, begin by giving a short sketch of the earlier religions of India.

PART I.

EARLIER RELIGIONS OF INDIA.

CHAPTER I.

EARLIEST VEDIC RELIGION.

Earliest records of religion in India.

THE earliest records we have of the Hindu religion, as of the Hindu race, are certain old hymns now known in their collected form as the Rig Veda. Of these the oldest are certainly not later than twelve hundred years before Christ, or more than three thousand years from the present date. They are important not only for the light which they cast on the early history of India, but also for that which they cast on the early history of mankind, and especially of that family to which English and Hindus alike belong, called from the word used in these hymns the Aryan race. The language in which they are written supplied the key to the relationship of the various languages spoken from Caithness to Cape Comorin, showing that they were originally one, and the peoples that speak them originally one tribe—that the Hindus are our brethren not merely as being members of the same human race, but as members of the same family of that race—that our common forefathers at one time dwelt together in the highlands of Central Asia; but the progenitors of the Hindus, after seeing their brethren go in successive emigrations westward to overrun and occupy Europe, by some unknown impulse turned south towards the sunny plains of India.

India three thousand years ago. The Aryas.

At the time these hymns were written the Aryas had advanced only as far as the Punjab and the banks of the Indus. They had but recently emigrated from a colder clime, for they reckoned their age by the number of their winters; and they still retained the fair complexion of their northern source. Their chief wealth seems to have consisted in flocks and herds, but they also practised agriculture largely. They had made considerable progress in the arts; they had built cities, and they traded in ships. Besides husbandmen and herdsmen, priests, warriors and merchants existed among them, but merely as professions, and not in any sense like the castes of modern India. Neither had they any particular rules about food: they even ate the flesh of the cow and praised it as the best of food. We can indeed trace among them scarcely any correspondence with the habits and customs of the Hindus as we now know them. But besides these Aryas there were also the Dasyus, of whom we learn little, but that they were dark in complexion, and constantly at war with the Aryas; they had also built cities and made some progress in civilization. Who they were I do not mean now to discuss. The word means natives[1] or nations. They were the inhabitants of India when the Aryas entered it, and bore to them much the same relation as the Gentiles did to the Jews or the Barbarians to the Greeks. It is well, however, to bear distinctly in mind that the first glimpses we get of India three thousand years ago reveals the ancestors of the present Brahmans, Rajputs and high

The Aborigines.

[1] H. H. Wilson, *Rig Veda*, vol. i. p. xlii.; Rev. Dr. Wilson, *India Three Thousand Years ago*, p. 19.

castes of India, living—a fair-complexioned race—in the north-west corner of the Peninsula, whither they had descended from the cool heights of the Himalayas, and all the rest of the Peninsula occupied by a darker and more savage race, the ancestors probably of the hill tribes and low castes, called by the Aryan conquerors then, as they are called by the English conquerors now, Dasyus—natives.

Religious beliefs.

On returning to the religious beliefs expressed in these hymns we get glimpses, or rather remains, of a pure primitive faith, but in the very earliest already draped in error, which in the later ones becomes grosser and more complete. It is possible that originally the various tribes of the Aryan race, ere they separated from each other, worshipped the one true God. But the proof for this is anterior to literature, and is derived entirely from philology.[2] By the time the earliest Sanskrit hymns were written, we find physiolatry, or nature-worship, obscuring Monotheism. The

Primitive Monotheism.

[1] Compare *deva* in Sanskrit with the Latin *deus* and Greek *theos*.

Aryas seem to have sought to realize the presence of God by naming Him after some of the noblest of His visible works. The hymns of the Vedas are addressed to various deities, whose names also express some of the phenomena of nature, or may be traced to them. But while this is the case, there is also evidence in the language that the worshipper originally looked 'from nature up to nature's God,' and sought to worship the Creator by the name of His works.

Two modes of expressing God.

It was a fine sentiment which led the Hebrew priests of old to omit the name of Jehovah in public worship, and substitute for it 'the incommunicable' or some such expression; for human language can never give a *name* to the Supreme. All that we have been able to do has been to take some attribute, and ascribe to it the other attributes of Deity. This will be found to be the case with nearly all the names which we employ, whether God—the good, Jehovah—the existent, the Eternal, the Lord, the Almighty, or the Supreme. All these are names which our moral consciousness testi-

By His attributes,

fies to us must be applicable to God; each describes only a part of His nature, but we think of it as comprehending the whole. This difficulty, which we have got over by taking an attribute for the possessor of that attribute, the old Aryas got over by taking

and by His works.

the work for the Maker—creation or part of creation for the Creator. These are the two currents of religious thought, originally little apart, which seem to have divided mankind when left to their own efforts to feel after and express God—the one looking at Him as concealed in the sanctuary of the human heart, the other as concealed behind the veil of nature. The former tendency was most clearly exemplified among the Jews, the latter among the Greeks and the Aryas of India.

Dyaus, the sky.

The visible object which most naturally calls out man's thoughts to a being above him is the sky or heaven, which in all languages is used also to designate the abode of the Supreme. But the Aryas went a step further and designated God from His abode. This seems to have been done before the various branches broke off from one another, before the Greeks went towards Greece or the Latins towards Italy; for the Greek *Zeus*, the Latin *Ju*piter, possibly our word *divine*, are explained by the Sanskrit root *dyu*, forming the noun *dyaus*, genitive *divas*. This is the name of one of the gods, possibly originally one of the names of the one God, but in Sanskrit it retains also its primitive meaning, which it has lost in all the other languages, namely, 'the sky or heaven.' By the time the earliest hymns were composed, he was conceived of as a distinct god, and the husband of Prithivi, the earth—heaven and earth being spoken of in them as the parents of all things.

Beyond the visible heaven the mind tries to imagine what may be, and the idea of the Infinite arises. This name Aditi is again identified with the Deity, and as all things are contained within it, it is personified as a goddess and the mother of all beings: of gods and men. In the Veda indeed its signification as an appellative has been lost, and it is used only as the name of a goddess, Aditi.

but in some of the addresses to her we can trace the influence of the original meaning, identifying her with everything, and thus sowing the seeds of Pantheism in the Indian mind. 'Aditi is the sky (dyaus); Aditi is the air; Aditi is the mother, and father, and son; Aditi is the collective gods; Aditi is the five persons;[3] Aditi is whatever has been born; Aditi is whatever is to be born.'

Varuna. The idea of the Infinite is calculated to produce in man a feeling of insignificance and consequent humility and fear; and we accordingly find Aditi addressed for forgiveness of sins. But there is one aspect of nature which more powerfully and immediately evokes such feelings, and that is the appearance of the nightly heavens. The 8th Psalm is perhaps the most devout and sublime expression of these sentiments which is to be found anywhere; but to them the Vedas owe some of their finest poetry, and the highest conception of God which is to be found in the first stage of Vedic re-

[3] Probably the same as the modern *panchàyat*, a court of five arbitrators.

ligion. The original name of this aspect of the heavens seems to have been Varuna.[4] By the time the Vedic hymns were written the meaning of the word as an appearance of nature had been entirely lost. It never occurs in them as a name of the sky, only as the name of a god; but in the hymns addressed to him we can trace the sentiment still ruling, which the gaze on the nightly heavens is calculated to rouse in the soul. The thousand stars have become in them the thousand eyes of the god, searching out all that passes on earth, from which even darkness cannot hide. The feelings of awe, sinfulness, and contrition remain in them, and make them liker the Hebrew Psalms than anything else in profane poetry. Here is one that irresistibly recalls the 139th Psalm. I give it in Dr. Muir's spirited metrical translation, which will bring the resemblance more vividly before English readers:—

[4] The same as the Greek *ouranos;* from a root meaning to cover. In the Vedas Varuna, as the god of night, is associated with Mitra, the god of the day. In later Hindu mythology he is the regent of the waters.

'The mighty Lord on high our deeds, as if at hand, espies:
The Gods know all men do, though men would fain their deeds disguise.
Whoever stands, whoever moves, or steals from place to place,
Or hides him in his secret cell—the Gods his movements trace.
Wherever two together plot and deem they are alone,
King Varuna is there, a third, and all their schemes are known.
The earth is his, to him belong those vast and boundless skies;
Both seas[5] within him rest, and yet in that small pool He lies.
Whoever far beyond the skies should think his way to wing,
He would not there elude the grasp of Varuna, the King.'[6]

In the following hymn we find the sentiment of guilt and the need of mercy more strongly expressed:—

'1. Let me not yet, O Varuna, enter the house of clay; have mercy, Almighty, have mercy!

'2. If I go along trembling, like a cloud driven by the wind, have mercy, Almighty, have mercy!

'3. Through want of strength, thou strong and bright God, have I gone to the wrong shore; have mercy, Almighty, have mercy!

[5] The waters above the firmament, and the waters under the firmament. See Gen. i. 7.

[6] Atharva V. iv. 16, *Sanskrit Texts*, v. p. 64.

'4. Thirst came upon the worshipper, though he stood in the midst of the waters; have mercy, Almighty, have mercy!

'5. Whenever we men, O Varuna, commit an offence before the heavenly host; whenever we break thy law through forgetfulness; have mercy, Almighty, have mercy.'[7]

The language of this hymn scarcely grates on the Christian sense, and if by Varuna we understand Him who dwells in heaven, little fault can be found with its theology. The same god is elsewhere addressed as 'Lord of All, of heaven and earth.' In the following verse, addressed also to him, we find the sentiment of the Psalmist, 'My soul thirsteth for Thee,' expressed by an external pastoral image:—

'Yearning for him, the far-seeing, my thoughts move onward as kine move to their pastures.'[8]

In the following prayer for forgiveness we find the germ of the tendency, now universal in India, to attribute sin to fate, contrasting strongly with the feeling of responsibility and guilt expressed in the Hebrew Psalms:—

[7] R. V. vii. 89. Trans. Max Müller's *Ancient Sanskrit Literature.*

[8] R. V. vii. 86. *Ibid.*

'Absolve us from the sins of our fathers and from those which we committed with our own bodies.

'It was not our own doing, O Varuna, it was necessity, an intoxicating draught, passion, dice, thoughtlessness. The old is near to mislead the young: even sleep brings unrighteousness.'[9]

Deterioration of religious ideas.

I have dwelt at some length on this for the illustration it affords of the relation of man to religion. If, as some maintain, his powers gradually developed and his ideas of God gradually rose, we should expect to find the oldest ideas of God in any literature the most degraded and obscure, and subsequent ones more gradually approaching the truth. Instead of this we find in the oldest hymns of India, with all their faults, the highest ideas of God, followed by constant deterioration. And the source of this deterioration is evident. It is the tendency to express God by His works. While the Hebrews, following the evidence of their moral consciousness, preserved the idea of the spirituality of God, till the hope of their nation—the 'Word made flesh'—presented to the world what it had vainly been feeling after, the Aryas, follow-

[9] R. V. vii. 86.

ing their observation of God's works, soon clothed their idea of Him with a material garb, which gravitated ever more rapidly to its earthly centre. They lost sight of the Creator and worshipped the creature, whether the phenomena of nature or the heroes of their nation. It is only in the very earliest hymns that we get a glimpse of the soul of nature-worship. In the later ones it is the mere body. It is noticed that the phenomena are distinct; hence the gods whom they represent are distinct also.

Worship of Indra, the rain god.

After the Aryas had entered the plains, and seen how by the blessing of the rain they were changed from dry sandy wastes to verdant pastures, that aspect of nature came to be of more importance to them, and was symbolized as Indra, whose worship superseded that of Varuna. He is the favourite god of the Vedas, though a later conception than those already named. He had from the beginning a more material character than the others; his birth is spoken of and in general the progress of anthropomorphism is visible. This is not to be wondered at. Even to persons less under the influence of natural phenomena than the Vedic bards, the approach of the monsoon sweeping over the plains, the piled clouds moving up in sharp distinction against the clear blue sky, with the lightning flashing beneath and the thunder rolling, readily suggests the idea of a king leading his hosts to battle.

Other gods. After Indra, Agni, the god of fire, manifested in the firmament as the sun, in the air as lightning, and on the altar as fire, was most revered, and he was especially the god of sacrifice. So too Vayu, the wind, Surya, the sun, and other objects of nature, were addressed as gods; and as conceptions of the Deity became more gross, a census of the gods, numbering thirty-three, was taken.

Each god supreme. There is, however, even in this early stage a marked difference between Indian and Greek mythology. In the latter the places and relations of the various gods are distinctly arranged; in the former the sentiment of there being one supreme God, who alone should be worshipped, seems to have remained, and made the worshippers of each god exalt him as such. In each hymn the god who is addressed is often spoken of as though he alone existed, and as though the writer were not conscious of any other. Sometimes he is expressly identified with others. 'Whatever we offer in repeated and plentiful oblations to any other deity is assuredly offered to thee (Agni).'[10] But, again, several gods are occasionally addressed in one hymn; and by degrees, as the conceptions become grosser, jealousies and quarrels take place among them. This is characteristic of the Hindu religion in the present day. Vishnu, Shiva, Ganpati, and other gods, are worshipped, but each is addressed by his worshippers as the supreme God.

The unknown God.

But alongside of this there was also a struggling after a retention of the conception of the one true God. While a daily deteriorating polytheism satisfied the majority, some more thoughtful minds recoiled from it, and, unable to find satisfaction elsewhere, looked to the unknown God. The following hymn is perhaps the most striking expression

[10] R. V. i. 2, 3, 6.

of this yearning of the mind to be found in any literature :—

'Then there was neither Aught nor Nought, no air nor sky beyond.
What covered all? Where rested all? In watery gulf profound?
Nor death was then, nor deathlessness, nor change of night and day,
That One breathed calmly, self-sustained; nought else beyond It lay.
Gloom hid in gloom existed first—one sea, eluding view,
That One, a void in chaos wrapt, by inward fervour grew.
Within It first arose desire, the primal germ of mind,
Which Nothing with Existence links, as sages searching find.
The kindling ray that shot across the dark and drear abyss,
Was it beneath? or high aloft? What bard can answer this?
There fecundating powers were found, and mighty forces strove,—
A self-supporting mass beneath and energy above.
Who knows, who ever told from whence this vast creation rose?
No gods had then been born—who then can e'er the truth disclose?
Whence sprang this world, and whether framed by hand divine or no,—
Its Lord in heaven alone can tell, if even he can show.'[11]

[11] R. V. x. 129. Trans. by Dr. Muir in *Sanskrit Texts*, vol. v.

Turning from the gods to the worship paid them, the following passage may be taken:— Early worship—sacrifice.

'We deprecate thy wrath with *prostrations*, with *sacrifice* and with *oblations;* averter of misfortune, wise and illustrious, be present amongst us, and mitigate the evils we have committed.

'Varuna, loose for me the upper, the middle, the lower band (of sin); so, son of Aditi, shall we, through faultlessness in thy worship, become freed from sin.'[12]

These verses show the kind of worship paid and its purpose. The object of the worshipper was to be freed from sin and to avert the wrath of God consequent thereon. For this purpose hymns were chanted, prostrations performed, and flowers and clarified butter offered in oblation; but the chief means to this end was the sacrifice, which was of four kinds—the goat, the cow, the horse, and man. This last is the most revolting feature in early Aryan worship, but it is one which we find in almost all ancient religions. The sacrifice of the horse seems to have been considered the most important, and is one rite which links the Aryas with northern tribes. As to *how* sacrifice delivered

Kinds of sacrifices.

[12] Wilson's *Rig Veda*, p. 64.

the sacrificer from sin we find no attempt at explanation till a later period; and I therefore defer further consideration of it. Of a future life the Aryas seem at first to have had no idea. Immortality seems afterwards to have been looked on as a gift that might be granted by the gods, but not an inherent property of man's nature. The good and virtuous man might attain to it, while annihilation awaited the sinner.[13] Future blessings they did not desire. The boons they asked of their gods were temporal gifts, abundance of cattle, increase of children, life to a good old age, freedom from pain, triumphing over their enemies. They seem, from their hymns, to have been a vigorous, hearty race, enjoying life, and living and acting only for the present.

Future life.

Religion of the aborigines.

In all this we find but little resemblance to modern Hinduism. But we must remember that this was the creed of the inhabitants of only a small corner of Hindustan. From the Sutlej to Cape Comorin were spread the Dasyus, tribes and nations of an alien race

[13] See Muir's *Sanskrit Texts*, vol. v. pp. 284, ff.

and alien religion, of which the Vedas take no account, but which has probably helped to mould Hinduism as much as the purer faith of the Aryas. Of the primitive religion of these tribes we have now no literary remains, the Tamil and Telugu literature having grown up since these nations were Brahmanized. But, judging from ruined monuments and from tradition, from the elements which we see conserved in Hinduism and from the present state of many aboriginal tribes, we may conclude that fetichism and devil-worship prevailed among the ruder tribes, and 'tree and serpent' and phallic worship among the more advanced. The whole of India was thus before the Aryas, a vast field for conquest and colonization, and for civilizing with their higher social and religious culture. How they fulfilled this mission we shall shortly see.

CHAPTER II.

BRAHMANISM.

Changes among the Aryas.

LET us now pass over a period of six hundred years to the time preceding the first great religious movement in India, which shook not only it, but all Asia to its utmost extremities. The Aryas have pushed forward their conquests as far as the Nerbudda, and have even effected settlements beyond it. Changes have come alike over their social system and their religion: Caste rules with its iron sway; a degraded polytheism and a rigid sacerdotalism have been developed from the original faith.

Origin of caste.

The origin of caste must be looked for in the relation of the Aryas to the conquered nations. Of these the most important was

The Sudras.

the Sudras—possibly the *Hudrakoi* of Herodotus. As in Europe, from numbers of the Sclavonic race being reduced to servitude, the name *esclave* or *slave* came to be applied to all bondmen, so in India the name Sudra came to be applied to all the conquered tribes. We know what a difference exists in any society between master and bondmen, especially when the latter are of a different race or of a different colour; and colour is the first meaning of the Hindi word for caste.[1] It is not so long since we have seen in a kindred state how low and degraded the condition of a subject race may become, even when modified by the presence of the Christian religion. We have seen how the words of the Bible may be twisted into supporting iniquities utterly opposed to its spirit; and we may imagine how vast the distinction between the rulers and the ruled would become, when a plastic religion lent itself to be moulded in the hands of the former to confirm their claims. The position assigned to the slaves by the laws of the Southern States of America, was noble compared with that, assigned to the Sudras by the old code of Manu. No Southern planter ever dreamt

[1] Varan.

of refusing to allow the negroes to be baptized; but in India, while the lordly Aryas were the *twice-born,* the Sudras were only the *once-born.* They could assume no sacred thread, the symbol of the second birth, admitting them to the privileges and hopes of religion, and they were menaced with death if they dared to engage in any of the acts of worship allowed to their superiors.

Position of the Sudras at the time of Ràma.

The following story from the Ràmàyana, one of the two old epic poems of India, will show the sentiment with which any attempts of the Sudras to rise into the religious sphere were then regarded. When Ràma was reigning happily in Ayodhya, the modern Oude, a Brahman came into his court one day and complained that the kingdom was under a curse owing to his heedless rule, adducing as a proof that his son just five years old had died. Ràma, unable to gainsay this evidence, proceeded, sword in hand, to search his kingdom to discover the cause. By the side of a lake he saw a man engaged in intense devotion, who, when interrogated, confessed himself to be a Sudra. For a servile man thus to seek admission to heaven was an iniquity quite sufficient to account for the calamity which had befallen the kingdom. Ràma by one stroke of his sword severed his head from his body, whereupon, it is added, the gods expressed their delight by showering down flowers, and the son of the Brahman was restored to life.

Subjection of the Sudras.

In accordance with such sentiments, the privileges of the twice-born were guarded by jealous legislation. If a twice-born man, for instance, abused one of the same caste, he was to be punished by a small fine; if a once-born man spoke disrespectfully of the caste of one of the twice-born, an iron style ten fingers long was to be thrust red hot into his mouth.

Origin of caste among the Aryas.

But this tyranny of race could not exist without reacting on the twice-born themselves. We know in America what a gap existed between the slave-owners and the poor whites, and so too class distinctions sprang up among the Aryas, though on quite different principles, and with much more inexorable rules. The language of the old hymns had become obsolete, and was known only to a class of men who had made it their business to study it, and who thus held the key to all religious service. These were the

Brahmans.

worshipping or praying ones, the Brahmans, who had come to be looked on as demigods, the highest of castes, safe in unapproachable sanctity. It was the greatest of all crimes to put them to death, and, therefore, of whatever crime they might be guilty, the utmost the king could do was to banish them from his kingdom. The

Kshatriyas.

warriors naturally imitated their religious teachers, and claimed privileges which the priests, who depended on them for protection, readily granted. They formed the second caste, with a position but little inferior to the Brahmans, while under them

Vaisyas.

the merchants and agriculturists formed the third caste. These were the three castes of the twice-born, while the whole of the Sudras, or once-born, were slumped together as the fourth caste.

Caste legislation.

The following is the account given in a

book of subsequent legislation to account for this division :—

'That the human race might be multiplied, he (Brahma) caused the Brahman, the Kshatriya, the Vaisya, and the Sudra to proceed from his mouth, his arm, his thigh, and his foot.'[2]

This is made the basis of legislation,—

'A once-born man who insults the twice-born with gross invectives ought to have his tongue slit; for he sprang from the lowest part of Brahma.'[3]

Each caste had its distinctive duties—the Brahmans to teach and to sacrifice; the Kshatriyas, or warriors, to rule and defend the people; the Vaisyas, or merchants, to trade and to tend cattle; the Sudras to serve the other three. The distinctions between them were sought to be maintained by strict laws about food and intercourse, and by restrictions upon intermarriage.

It will be seen from this account that the Brahmans. Brahmans were at the head of the social system, and that it was their knowledge of the old hymns which was the foundation of their superiority. This knowledge had different effects, as it always will have on

[2] Inst. of Manu, i. 31. [3] *Ib.* viii. 270.

different minds. Some used it as a means of impressing their superiority on the more ignorant. Others were led into deeper speculation as to the meaning of what they learned. Hence arose the two classes, Brahman priests and Brahman sages.

Priests. The former developed an elaborate ceremonial of sacrifice, that tended to surround them with religious awe. The ancient hymns were gathered into the collection known as the Rig Veda, and two other Vedas were compiled by selections from it —one called the Yajur Veda, the liturgy of a lower order of priests, to whom was intrusted the material part of the sacrifice; and the other, called the Sàma Veda, the hymn book of a higher order of priests, who sang in chorus at certain points during its performance. The Sanskrit word for these hymns is *Mantra*, which in Hindi and in Modern Sanskrit means a charm. Some of these charms consist of parts of the hymns of the Rig Veda, which the Brahmans now use without having the slightest idea of their meaning or of whence they are derived. A fourth Veda, called the Atharva, was afterwards added, more as a collection of charms than to aid in sacrifice.[4]

The Brahmanas.

It would be tedious to enter into all the details of ceremonial which were at this time instituted, and which were all calculated to surround the Brahmans with a halo of sanctity and power. Attached to each of the Vedas a new literature sprang up, called the Brahmanas, professing to be a sort of rubric for the use of the Vedas during the sacrifice; but in reality containing many additional commands or stories. They may be considered the priestly literature of the age, and they show in a striking manner the blighting effect which their assumed power and priestly formalism had on the minds of the Brahmans themselves. 'No one would have supposed that at so early a period and in so primitive a state of society, there could have

[4] Many of the hymns in the Atharva Veda are probably as old as any in the Rig Veda; but they are collected for an entirely different purpose, for imprecation, and not sacrifice. The beautiful hymn quoted p. 20 is found in the Atharva, but it is there degraded into an introduction to an imprecation. —See Prof. Roth, in Muir's *Sanskrit Texts*, vol. v. p. 64.

risen up a literature which for pedantry and downright absurdity can hardly be matched anywhere. . . . It is most important to the historian that he should know how soon the fresh and healthy growth of a nation can be blighted by priestcraft and superstition. It is most important that we should know that nations are liable to these epidemics in their youth as well as in their dotage. These works deserve to be studied as the physician studies the twaddle of idiots and the raving of madmen. They will disclose to a thoughtful eye the ruins of faded grandeur, the memories of noble aspirations. But let us only try to translate these works into our own language, and we shall feel astonished that human language and human thought should ever have been used for such purposes.'[5]

Development of polytheism. On turning to the ideas of God exhibited in these and other records, we see one result of the first error of expressing the Deity by His works—a great development of polytheism. The original meaning

[5] Max Müller, *Ancient Sanskrit Literature*, p. 389.

of the names of the gods of the Vedas had with the change of language been lost, and the phenomena were now looked on as persons. Some had dropped out of worship, and others had assumed a foremost place. Indra was still one of the principal gods, but Vishnu, a very inferior god in the Vedas, was coming to dispute his supremacy. An entirely new god, Bràhmà, had appeared. The origin of the conception of this god cannot now be determined, but the name seems to have originated with the Bràhmans, and they as his worshippers seem to have been called after him. Brăhmăn means prayer or sacred rite, and Brăhmà, he of prayer. It was possibly a name given originally to whatever god was honoured in sacrifice, and we find him identified with other gods. The root however means also increase, and we find Brahmà more definitely conceived of as the Creator. Some of the myths with regard to him are merely gross conceptions of the process of creation. He is sometimes represented as producing the universe from an egg, and sometimes by

Brahmà.

separating himself into male and female. He was specially the god of the Brahmanical caste, but he never came to be popular with the other castes. As old gods assumed new places, or new ones were created, fresh myths, grown constantly more sensuous, gathered around them.

Brahmanical and Levitical sacrifices.

It will already be seen that at this period sacrifice was the great centre of religion. It was as priests of sacrifice that the Brahmans obtained their power, and in connection with sacrifice that the sacred hymns were sung. The word itself, *yajna* or *yàga*,[6] preserves the sacred significance attached to the act in primitive worship; and some of its principal features corresponded closely with those which gave significance to sacrifice under the Levitical law. I give these as they are epitomized by Mr. Hay in the *Indian Evangelical Review*.

[6] 'The memory of the sacredness of the yajna or yàga, from yàja to worship, has been preserved and handed down to us in the *hagno* and *hagio* of the Greeks; and probably also in the *sacer* of the Latins (= sak with the formative affix er), *y*, *h*, and *s* being exchangeable according to well-ascertained laws of etymology.'—Rev. John Hay, in *Ind. Ev. Rev.*, *Jan.* 1874.

'*a.* It was substitutionary. "The sacrificer ransomed himself by it."[7] "The sacrificer is the animal."[8] "The animal is as it were ransoming the man."[9]

'*b.* The yajna was the means of liberation from sin and death. "Those who sacrifice remove their sin."[10] "Them all"—*i.e.* the thousand lethal ropes of death—"by the power of sacrifice we sacrifice away."[11] "He who sacrifices propitiates the gods."[12]

'*c.* It secured heaven. "What is offered by fire is an offering relating to heaven."[13] "Let him who desires heaven sacrifice." "Sacrifice is the ship that ferrieth over."[14]

'*d.* The yajna was offered by faith. "By faith the fire of sacrifice is kindled; by faith the offering is offered."[15] "By faith and truth together they gain the heaven world."'[16]

These passages, similar to many more that might be quoted, show that the Brahmans attached to their sacrifices a significance not very different from that which we now attach to the old Levitical sacrifices. Still more startling is the point of difference between the two. The latter was typical, the former sacramental. The utter impossibility that 'the blood of bulls and of goats should take away sins,' is a truth that must be felt by every one who realizes

Difference between them.

[7] Ait. Br. ii. 3.
[8] Tait. Br. ii. 8, 2.
[9] Tait. Sam. vi. 1, 11, 6.
[10] Ait. Br. v. 25.
[11] Tait. Br. xi. 2, 2, 5.
[12] S. P. Br. i. 9, 1, 3.
[13] Ait. Br. i. 16.
[14] Ait. Br. i. 13.
[15] R. V. x. 151, 1; Tait. Br. ii. 8, 8, 6.
[16] Ait. Br. vii. 10.

what sin is. Making an animal the involuntary substitute for man to atone for his guilt is shocking to man's idea of God's holiness and justice. It is only the fact of a primitive divine institution that can account for this universal mode of man's expressing his desire for peace with God, and only the supposition of its being symbolical that can account for its institution. But what did it symbolize? The Hebrews felt more than any others its utter inadequacy, and at the same time more than any others persisted in a simple observance of it, as it had been instituted, without attempting any explanation of its hidden meaning.

Levitical sacrifices typical.

> 'For Thou desirest not sacrifice, else would I give it:
> Thou delightest not in burnt-offering.
> The sacrifices of God are a broken spirit;
> A broken and a contrite heart, O Lord, Thou wilt not despise.'[17]

Thus the Psalmist expresses the convictions of his conscience as to the inadequacy of mere sacrifice; but again, in the conviction that it had been divinely appointed, he adds—

[17] Psa. li. 16, 17.

'Then shalt Thou be pleased with the sacrifice of righteousness,
With burnt-offerings and whole burnt-offerings;
Then shall they offer bullocks upon Thine altar.'[18]

The same antagonism may be observed constantly throughout the Psalms and the prophets—conscience struggling against faith; man's sense of what is right and of what is due to God protesting against an ordinance of God which it cannot understand. But with the Jews faith prevailed; they accepted the institution simply, without trying to put into it anything of their own; and by degrees the idea of the Antitype was developed. Isaiah in vision saw One who, like the sacrificial lamb, was to bear the sins of His people. At length, in the death of Christ on Calvary, the whole course of Jewish sacrifice was fulfilled, and since then it has ceased. Then it was shown that divine power alone can bear man's sins, that sacrifice is effectual only when Deity is present in it.

But well-nigh a thousand years before the coming of Christ, the Brahmans of India had felt, and in their own way expressed, this Brahmanical sacrifices sacramental.

[18] Psa. li. 19.

truth. Conscious seemingly that the animal sacrificed could not of itself bear the sin that it was to atone for, or accomplish the work that by its offering was to be accomplished, they boldly declared that God Himself was in the animal sacrificed, and that thus it was efficacious. In this respect Brahmanical sacrifice was sacramental rather than typical; it resembled the sacrifice of the host in the Roman Catholic Church rather than the Levitical sacrifice. The Creator, under the name of Prajapati, is said thus to be offered in sacrifice, and how this is possible is explained with a subtlety that a Jesuit apologist might envy.

'Prajapati is this sacrifice. Prajapati is both of these two things, uttered and unuttered, finite and infinite. What the priest does with the Yajus text, with that he consecrates the form of Prajapati which is uttered and finite. And what he does silently with that he consecrates the form of Prajapati which is unuttered and infinite.'[19]

But it is more frequently Vishnu that is thus spoken of. He is said to have become incarnate in the animal slain—to have become incarnate in order to be sacrificed, and

[19] Muir's *Sanskrit Texts*, vol. v. p. 393.

by his sacrifice to have become the greatest of the gods.

'Then the gods said, "Whoever among us, through toil, austerity, faith, sacrifice and oblation, first comprehends the issue of the sacrifice, let him be the most eminent of us; this shall be common to us all." To this they consented, saying, "Be it so." Vishnu first attained the proposed object. He became the most eminent of the gods. . . . He who is this Vishnu is sacrifice; he who is this sacrifice is Vishnu.'[20]

This idea has never been entirely forgotten, and even in the latest of the Puranas, the Bhagavata, sacrifice is given as one of twenty-two incarnations of Vishnu. Amid all the puerilities and absurdities of the texts relating to this subject, the truth sought after must not be lost sight of.

Difficulties in this view.

But this only increased the original difficulty, and by seeking a premature fulfilment of sacrifice hastened its rejection by India altogether. If it was difficult to believe that an animal could bear man's sin, it was much more difficult to believe that it could be God. We know the repugnance of some earnest, philosophic minds to accept the idea

[20] For this and similar texts see Muir's *Sanskrit Texts*, vol. iv. pp. 121-129.

that Christ was God, even though they exhaust the powers of human language in praise of His Godlike character. So too the idea that God was sacrificed as an animal could not but provoke a reaction and alienate the best thought of the country. It was an idea that could consist only with a blind and tyrannical sacerdotalism, which it helped to exalt, but which it must also help to destroy.

Brahman sages.

We find, accordingly, alongside of this ritualistic development a rationalistic development, the records of which, called the Upanishads, may be looked on as the literature of the Brahman sages, as the Brahmanas are that of the priests. They are the only parts of the Vedas now extensively read in India. They come at the end of the Vedas, and are therefore called Vedant (Veda end); whence the name of the most influential school of modern Hindu philosophy, which professes to be founded on them. It would be hard to say what philosophical opinion might not be supported on their authority, for the most contradictory statements find a place in them, yet the

Upanishads.

tendency is on the whole towards pantheism. Pantheism. We have seen that the original error of expressing God by His works developed, on the one hand, into erecting each of the natural phenomena into distinct gods, and thus led to polytheism. In the Upanishads, on the other hand, we see the same error developing into confounding God with His works and His works with God. In the earlier hymns of the Vedas, too, when polytheism had made some way, the worshippers of each individual god sought to exalt it to the position of the one God, by identifying it with other gods, and even with creation. What was at first merely figurative was afterwards viewed as real, what was at first mysticism was afterwards considered perfect philosophy. We find accordingly, in the latter parts of the Vedas, attempts to explain on a rational basis all the poetical figures of the former parts. In one place it is stated that Self or Spirit alone existed, and he thought let me create the worlds, and he created these worlds. Again delusion is called the great principle, and this world the effect of delusion on the Spirit, while elsewhere delusion is called one of the powers of Spirit. In a word, we find much pantheistic thought but no pantheistic philosophy. The elements existed, but they had not been systematized.

Origin of metempsychosis.

One result of this process of thought was modifying the belief in a future state into the doctrine of the transmigration of souls. This doctrine, which makes a man in a future birth atone for the errors of this, strikes at the root of the original idea of sacrifice; but as it is only in modern Hinduism that we find it fully developed, I defer the consideration of it, merely noting that at this time it first appeared on the horizon of Hindu thought and religion. One consequence which it had was the growth of asceticism and the practice of austerities. When happiness in a future state was made to depend on a man's exertions in his present state, it naturally led him to seek to be free from those attachments which might lead him into incurring guilt, and this led again to giving up the plain duties of life for meditation and

Asceticism.

penance. These came at last to be exalted by some as superior to everything else. Self-denial was sublimated into self-torture, and became the most generally accepted symbol of sanctity.

Effect of philosophy on religion.

These two currents of thought—pantheism and polytheism, philosophy and sacerdotalism—could not, in such a country as India, co-exist without interpenetrating one another. The demon of heresy had not yet appeared, the sages and ascetics professed to be devout worshippers of the gods, and the priests adapted their religion to the ideas of the philosophers with a consistent logic such as could be witnessed in no country but India. It was natural enough that they should take advantage of the doctrine of transmigration by prescribing ceremonies and purifications to attain beatitude in a future state of existence. It was natural enough, too, that they should not be behindhand in the practice of those austerities, which gave them an odour of sanctity with the people and of ridicule with the sceptics. But what shall we say of their declaring austerities to be the source of the power of the gods themselves [21]—the origin of their very divinity, of their calling even the sacrifice of Vishnu an act of penance performed to gain power? When religion had reached this point it had evidently run to seed and was smitten with decay.

Other sources of religious ideas.

Thus, by the disintegration and reintegration of ideas, we see that many of the elements of modern Hinduism had already been developed out of the primitive faith of the Vedas. But other elements were imported from other sources. While the Brahmans had been drivelling and speculating, the Kshatriyas, the warrior caste, had been fighting and conquering. In one conflict, indeed, they seem to have been worsted. They did not at once yield to the Brahmans the superiority which they desired without a bloody struggle. The details of it are altogether lost to us, and the results epitomized with an exaggeration which subsequent events prove to have been altogether false. But this much is known, that a great war-

Struggle between Brahmans and Kshatriyas.

[21] *Sanskrit Texts,* vol. iv. p. 181; vol v. p. 15.

rior, called Parasu Rama—possibly himself a Brahman—espoused the cause of the Brahmans, and fought against the Kshatriyas with such success that, in later myths, he is said three times to have extirpated them from the earth. At all events, after this the Brahmans were left undisturbed in their religious and social superiority—the counsellors, the priests, the gods of the warriors and kings, while these were carving out the history of their people.

Rama's expedition to Ceylon.

Two great events belong to this period. The first is the expedition of Rama Chandra from Oudh to Ceylon to recover his wife Sita, who had been carried off by the king of that island. On the way he had to encounter many of the savage or semi-civilized tribes south of the Nerbudda, and with many of them he formed alliances. He triumphed at last over Ravana, king of Ceylon, and returned with his wife to Oudh. This was the first great expedition of the Aryas to the south, and it is imprinted indelibly on the Hindu mind. It became the theme of song—a mass of tradition and exaggeration gathered round it, and in after-ages it became the subject of an epic poem, the Ramayana, which, though full of absurdities and overlaid with Brahmanical conceits, yet contains some of the purest and noblest thoughts to be found in profane poetry.

Legend of the Pandavs and Krishna.

The second great fact was the struggle for supremacy between two rival Kshatriya races, the Pandavs and the Kauravs. After a bloody war the former triumphed, with the assistance of Krishna, a celebrated Indian prince and hero, and their rivals were destroyed. This has produced an even greater impress on the mind of India than the former. Three-fourths of the Hindus are ignorant of all that has happened since. The rise and fall of Buddhism, the rise and fall of Mahommedanism, even the progress of the English by whom they are now ruled, are for them blank pages of history; but the adventures of the Pandav brothers, two thousand five hundred years ago—their misfortunes, their patience, their sufferings, their ultimate triumph, and the valour of their great ally Krishna, are present realities for them, and still, as they are yearly recited at their festivals, melt them into tears, move them into laughter, or excite them to triumph with all the intensity of personal interest. The poem in which their deeds are preserved, the Mahabharat, has been so encrusted with later additions of the Brahmans, didactic pieces, extraneous traditions, and episodes, that it is now almost impossible to say what the original poem was. But we may safely conclude that, at the time of which we are speaking, the exploits of these warriors were sung and heard with an interest not inferior to that which they now excite; and thus the foundation was being laid of hero-worship, which afterwards came to exercise such an important influence on Hinduism.

Hero-worship.

Aboriginal worship.

And there was yet another element which, though altogether latent in so far as extant literature is concerned, we must believe existed with an extent and power which subsequent revolutions fully showed. All that we have been considering, in so far as religion, philosophy, and history are concerned, relates only to the twice-born. The once-born Sudras were out of the pale altogether, and considered unfit for any religious exercise or worship. Yet we cannot but suppose that they sought God after their own fashion—that they had a religion, a worship of their own, which their lords might ignore, but which was afterwards to throw its yoke over their own heads. We may suppose that most of the Sudras, the majority of the population of India, worshipped their own fetishes and deities, trees and serpents, stones and idols. Already they were beginning to exercise some effect on the upper castes, for we find the worship of images noticed in Manu.

Summary. Such, then, was the state of society before Buddhism appeared in India. An inexorable caste system consigned the bulk of the people to a grinding slavery and hopeless perdition, while it exalted the priesthood to the level of the gods, and left the warriors to fight and rule, and the merchants to trade and get gain—both to indulge in luxury and sensuality to the extent of their power. A debasing sacerdotalism had been impregnated with a sceptical philosophy, which needed only to be dissociated from it to ensure its overthrow. It must not be supposed that this represented the society of the whole of India at that time. It represents only the Brahmanical conception of society: what the Brahmans had made it where their power was established, and what they wished to make it throughout India. But their power was fully established only in a few parts—in others it was less so, and in others not at all. The Sudras in some parts might be able to assert their equality even with the Brahmans, and for whole nations these latter would be but foreign priests. The two opposite extremes of consolidated Brahmanism and undisturbed aboriginal worship existed, and between the two every shade of opinion existed in a seething, unsettled state—a fertile soil for a new and strong religion to take root in.

Extent of Brahmanism.

CHAPTER III.

BUDDHISM.

Buddha's birth.

BUDDHA, or Gotama, to whom Buddhism owes its rise, was born about six hundred years before our era,[1] in the city of Kapila Vastu, the capital of a kingdom at the foot of the Himalayas, of which his father was king. The family or clan to which he belonged was the Sakya, one of the divisions of the Kshatriya or warrior caste. His mother, Maya, died seven days after he was born, an event the knowledge of which in after-life is said to have produced a great effect on him. He early showed a predilection for meditation and seclusion, which probably led the astrologers to predict that he would one day leave his kingdom and become an anchorite. His father, to prevent this,

[1] Buddha died at the age of 80. The date of his death is usually fixed at 543 B.C.; but Max Müller has advanced strong reasons for fixing it at 477 B.C.

urged him to marry, and demanded for him the hand of a beautiful princess. The prince yielded to his father's solicitations, and, according to Kshatriya custom, conquered in combats of various kinds the other competitors for the hand of the princess, ere he married her.

Married life.

Some years of his life passed in the married state, and it is not improbable that he, during them, yielded to the seductions and luxury which characterize Eastern courts, and with which tradition represents him to have been surrounded, though it also represents him as uncontaminated by them. It is more natural to suppose that he did yield to the temptations with which he was beset, but, doing so against the natural bent of his mind, a feeling of nausea and disgust was fomented, which ultimately exploded and drove him to burst asunder all restraints, and give himself up to the opposite extreme of asceticism. The occasion of this change in his life, and in the whole religious history of the East, was the following:—One day, when he was driving as usual to his pleasure-

Change caused by seeing age,

garden, he saw a man covered with wrinkles, scarcely able to speak from feebleness, walking tremblingly along, leaning on his staff. He asked the driver who that man was. The charioteer replied that he was a man suffering from old age, and the consequent decay of all his powers. 'Is that a condition to which he and his family alone are liable, or all mankind?' asked the prince. 'He is no exception,' replied the charioteer; 'all must fall into age and decrepitude.' 'Then drive my chariot home again,' said the prince; 'what have I to do with pleasure who am the future abode of age and decay!' On another day he met a loathsome leper, and learned from his charioteer that all men were liable to disease. On a third occasion he saw a dead body, and learned that death is the end of all men. All happiness in his life of luxury had fled, and he set himself to ponder how he might escape the woes of which he had been witness. As he was driving out on a fourth occasion he saw a recluse, and learned from his charioteer that he was a man who had

Disease,

Death,

and a recluse.

renounced this world's wealth and pleasure, lived on alms, and spent his time in meditation. This suggested to the prince how he might attain his end: he did not return at once to his home, but drove on to the garden with his mind at ease and settled, and then returned to the palace.

He renounces royalty.

That same night his wife had given birth to her first-born son. He went to take a farewell look of her and of the babe lying in her breast; but, fearful lest his resolution might fail, he tore himself away, and calling on his groom to saddle his horse, and taking him as his only companion, he left the palace and rode all night through the forest. When morning dawned he gave his horse and best robes to the groom, and sent him back with a message to his father and wife not to follow and seek him, 'for,' said he, 'I will not return till I can bring them tidings of deliverance.' Then he assumed the garb of a mendicant, and set out on his quest to find a way of deliverance from age, disease and death.

Brahmanism does not seem to have been

Studies with the Brahmans.

dominant at Kapila Vastu, and Gotama's first religious impulses were independent of it. He had settled in his mind the main object of all religion before he came in contact with the teaching of the Brahmans, and thus brought to it a mind free to observe and to criticize. But they were the holders of the holy mysteries, and to them he turned first for instruction. Some of their teaching evidently affected him, but he soon saw that they were blind leaders of the blind. Their ideas of transmigration and works he could assent to, but he saw that the gods whom they worshipped were no gods, that a power obtained by austerity was but the same power as man could gain, and did not entitle them to adoration. Sacrifice he saw to be a hollow sham, and as causing pain and death to an animate being it was abominable to him. The end of religion, he had decided, was mercy, and was valueless if it could not assuage or remove human misery.

Retires to the forests.

Dissatisfied with their teaching, he retired, with five Brahmans who accompanied him, to the forests, to seek how he might gain this great end. This led to his getting the name of Sakya Muni (the Sakya sage or recluse), by which he is most generally known in India. In his retreat he beheld those same great objects of nature by which the early Aryas had named their gods, and which they had come to deify; but their faith had now run its course, had been tried and found wanting. He looked on them all only as things which must pass away and perish, and they became for him the greatest symbols of dissolution. He saw that the wild beasts of the forest paid no more respect to him, a king's son, than to the meanest outcast, and he was thus led to see the utter vanity of all caste distinctions. He turned to his own thoughts to see what they could teach him, and continued six years to afflict himself with fasting, but he found no solution of his difficulty, and all his strength was wasting away. He resolved at last to change his plan and take more food. This seemed to his Brahman followers relapsing into worldliness; they returned to Benares, and left him alone to solve the problem of humanity. He was nearly on the point of giving up the search, but again he took with him food enough to support him for forty-nine days, took up his position beneath a mimosa tree, and gave himself up to severe meditation. He had, while there alone, to endure a frightful mental struggle. Temptations came thick upon him; demons, according to the after legend, assailed him, and he had to maintain sore conflicts with them. But at length he was triumphant, and he saw what he had been searching for. The four verities that constituted the way of deliverance rose clearly before him.[2]

He discovers the way of deliverance,

He had now obtained for himself the desired knowledge, and had he been as other sages he might have been satisfied with this, and his name and influence been lost to the East. But the mind of Buddha was intensely human; sympathy with the sufferings of man was what prompted him to undergo all the hardships he had undergone, and he felt that his knowledge would be valueless if it did not benefit his fellows. He had to pass

[2] See Appendix A, Buddha's System.

through another conflict before he could make up his mind to this; but at last he triumphed, and was prepared to bring deliverance to the world. He sought out the five Brahmans who had originally accompanied him, and told them the truths he had discovered. He sought out his Brahman preceptors, but found to his grief that many of them had died without the knowledge of final deliverance; so he turned to teach those that remained. His doctrines spread with rapidity; kings even became his followers. He returned to Kapila Vastu, and taught his doctrines to his father, wife, and all his family; and they too became his disciples. Yet he never swerved from the manner of life he had chosen; he continued a recluse, without a single worldly possession, refusing even to ask for food, but taking with contentment whatever was given him. So he went about from city to city and village to village, till he was eighty years of age, when one day, having partaken of some unwholesome food that had been given him, and having walked a long distance after, he was

and communicates it to others.

seized with dysentery, and died, or, as the Buddhists say, entered Nirvana.

Connection between his life and religion.

I have given these details of Buddha's life, for, without knowing them, it is impossible to appreciate his religion or understand the rapid success which it had. It is not exclusively the offspring of his own intuitions, nor is it a mere modification of Brahmanical theology. It is rather the result of a review of that system by an independent mind of pure moral tone, deep, human sympathies and fearless logic. He had formed his conception of man's needs before he resorted to the Brahmans, and when he found their teaching unsatisfying, he fled to the woods, and for six years the lessons he had heard from them matured in the soil of his intense feeling and experience; and the result was Buddhism.

Transmigration.

The key-stone of this system, as conceived in the mind of its founder, was the transmigration of souls. This was really the only point of contact between it and Brahmanism. He accepted this doctrine as the only solution of the miseries and inequalities of this life. Present joy was the reward of good deeds in a previous birth, present sorrow the punishment of previous sin; while present virtue and vice would be requited in future births. A man's future state thus depended on his own works; therefore, he deduced, it did not depend on any divine will. We have seen that already in Brahmanism the gods were by some considered to have attained their divinity by religious austerities. This view Buddha accepted in a modified sense; but he drew from it the conclusion that they were in no sense better than men. They were the inhabitants of the heavens, as the devils were of the hells, fish of the waters, men and animals of the earth. They had gained their high position by good deeds, but they were liable to decay, and might again become mortals or beasts. Their high state was one to be comparatively desired, but to worship such beings was an absurdity. In the same way he could conceive no Supreme Being influenced by worship; that would have been to suppose him liable to motives, desire, and consequent

Gods no gods.

Atheism.

decay. Thus he, with terrible logic, excluded God from his system, not absolutely denying His existence, but ignoring it, and constructing a religion independent of Him. But could he have constructed anything better out of the system which the Brahmans gave him?

Nirvàna.

He thus looked on a universe without God—this world, with a series of hells beneath for the punishment of the wicked, and of heavens above for the reward of the good, to which spirits were sunk or raised by their own acts, but in no one of which could they permanently continue. Decay would seize them, and quit it they must, to enter on a similar course of birth and decay in another state. To be quit of all this was the end to which men should ultimately look; but to be quit of this was to be quit of existence. Final quiescence and final annihilation are thus equally the meaning of Nirvàna, the Buddhist *summum bonum.*

Better elements of his system.

Up to this point we see Brahmanism working its own destruction, leading a logical mind to utter nihilism. Buddha had thus cut himself off from God; but in the rest of his system we see the better part of his nature, his moral purity, and strong human sympathy gradually asserting itself, and leading to a system of benevolence and philanthropy so thorough, as to seem to show that the loss of one pole of religious thought —God—had developed with all the greater intensity and even excess the attraction of the other pole of religion—man, or rather living creatures.

Way of deliverance.

In pointing out the way to Nirvàna he could not shake himself altogether free from his false conception of it. Considering pain to be caused by affections and desires, he taught that it could be removed only by the removal of affection and desire. Negation of God led thus directly to negation of humanity. Having deprived man of the object of his desires, of an eternal God to satisfy them fully and eternally, he could cure the longing only by destroying it. But, in the method to lead to this annihilation of desire, we see his better nature coming out. The best way he indeed taught

Asceticism.

to be, becoming a recluse and practising meditation, which might conduct the mind to a quietude nearly approaching Nirvàna. But the Buddhist recluses had none of the repulsiveness of the Brahman recluses, and they were not freed from duties of benevolence. Becoming recluses, however, was not a religion adapted for all men. He therefore taught the laity to seek rather to secure a happy condition in their next birth, entrance to heaven, or a state on earth which would allow of their becoming recluses, and give them a hope of entering Nirvàna.

Religion for the laity.

Morality.

It is here that the immense superiority of his system to that of the Brahmans appears. They taught that this end was to be attained by austerity and penance, or by sacrifice and other religious ceremonies, which had become empty forms. Buddha having rejected God, could not accept worship as a means; he therefore adopted works, but he taught that these works were not penance, but fulfilling the moral law—which he taught both negatively and positively,—practising charity and benevolence towards all animated beings;

honesty, chastity, truthfulness, and temperance. It is the glory of Buddhism that it has asserted this law as the great law of religion.

Another excellence which it owes to Buddha's strong benevolence is, that it abolishes the distinction of caste. This might seem to be a natural consequence of the Brahmanical doctrine of metempsychosis; for if the spirit of a Brahman may be a Sudra in next birth and a Chandala in the subsequent one, why should there be any difference between these castes at all? We shall see, however, in treating of Hinduism, that this doctrine may be made to teach the very opposite, and if this reasoning were carried out, it would show that there is no difference between man and the animals. It was probably the strong common sense and intense human sympathy of Buddha that made him reject the doctrine of caste, and receive all men as brethren. No doubt the psychological argument—the transmigration of souls—might have some influence with him, and it was this probably that led him to lay so much stress on the

Abolition of caste.

Tenderness to the brute creation.

duty of preserving animal life, which has in subsequent developments of his religion come to overshadow even duty to man. Thus this humanitarianism, which is the chief glory of Buddhism, being disjoined from worship of God, has been betrayed into an excess which tends even to lower man.

Worship of relics.

But man cannot live without some object of worship. Even the author of Positivism in France found this, and tried to invent a worship having as its object woman in her threefold relation of mother, wife and daughter. So, too, the greater author of a greater system more than two thousand years ago found that he needed an object of worship. One of his dearest friends having been killed by some of his enemies, he preserved some relics of him with a care and devotion amounting to worship, and thus the worship of relics was introduced into Buddhism. The central object of worship in Buddhist temples is a tomb in which relics are supposed to be.

Spread of Buddhism and its causes.

Such was the system which Buddha expounded, and which soon began to spread throughout India with a rapidity that even its intrinsic superiority to its rival, Brahmanism, can scarcely account for. It did indeed appeal to a law which was confirmed by the law in the hearts of all men, and it set before the multitude of its adherents an end which they could easily understand—a future happy birth as a reward of good conduct and obedience to the law. But we cannot doubt that the character of its founder contributed greatly to its spread. Mistaken he may have been, and the desertion of his wife and child was certainly reprehensible, but we must recollect that he had been forced into these relationships against his natural inclinations and conscientious desire, and he felt impelled by an inward call which he could not resist. Having once set out on his career as a religious inquirer and teacher, he showed himself earnest, self-denying, self-sacrificing. He is the one example of a human teacher who in his life was more than his religion. Whatever he might call on his followers to do, he had done more. None of them could renounce more than he had renounced,

Character of the founder.

none of them could endure greater hardships and privations than he had endured. The spectacle of him renouncing all that man most prizes; going into the desert, and agonizing there for six years; and at last, alone and deserted, without even a ray of hope in a God to cheer him, withstanding all the temptations that came on him, working out his conception of man's deliverance; then hastening, in overflowing sympathy, to communicate it to all who would hear him; and, when he had attracted thousands of followers, still continuing the poorest of the poor,—is one of the grandest pictures of self-denial and service which the world has produced, and was a constant testimony before all men to the sincerity of his convictions, the depth of his sympathy. Let us try to imagine what must have been the effect of this example on the downtrodden Sudras and low castes, who had been trained to believe that they were beyond the pale of religion, that they merited death if they sought to hear the sacred books read, or to perform any of the religious acts of the twice-born—to be told that there was no difference between them and their lords—to find themselves welcomed to instruction in the mysteries of religion, no difference being made between the lowest and the highest if there was but a sincere desire for the truth—to learn that there was but one way of deliverance for the high caste and the out-caste, for the Brahman and the Sudra. They saw all that he had endured to do them this good, and they could say, though in an altogether earthly sense, 'though he was rich, yet for our sakes he became poor.' What must the effects of this have been on all those among the higher castes who had any noble or generous feelings left? When we remember all this we may cease to wonder at the effect which his life and teaching had.

Buddhism a religion of humanity.

Buddhism not only rose above caste; it rose above nationality. It was the first religion of humanity. The germs of Christianity were indeed contained in Judaism. Long before this time the Jews had sung in the Temple service,—

'God be merciful unto us and bless us, and cause His face to shine upon us;

'That Thy way may be known upon earth, Thy saving health among all nations.'

But it was not till six hundred years after Buddha that this seed fructified, and He in whom Judaism was fulfilled gave the command, 'Go ye into all the world, and preach the Gospel to every creature.' Buddha was the first to teach a religion which might be common to all men, and to seek to awaken in man's heart the idea of a brotherhood as broad as the human race. In spreading his doctrines he had but one instrument—persuasion. Subsequent legends do represent him as performing miracles, but this was a power which he himself disclaimed. When urged by a king to perform miracles so as to confound his enemies, he replied, 'The law which I teach my disciples is not—Go before the Brahmans, and by the help of supernatural power perform miracles greater than men can perform. The law I give them is this—Be silent about your good deeds, and confess your sins.' He likewise repudiated all force or constraint in spreading

Persuasion his sole instrument.

his doctrine. Even when the most powerful kings had become his disciples, and were ready to put their armies at his disposal, he refused all means but persuasion and teaching; and in this respect Buddhists have obeyed the teaching of their master better than Christians have obeyed the teaching of theirs.[3] His own example, however, inspired many to become missionaries of his religion with a devotedness like his own. The following legend may serve as an illustration:—

His example.

A rich merchant of the name of Purna had become a convert to Buddha's teaching, and, renouncing all his wealth, resolved to fix his abode among a neighbouring savage tribe, whom he wished to convert to the law. Buddha at first tried to discourage him.

Legend of Purna.

'The men of Sronaparanta, whither thou wilt go,' he said to him, 'are violent, cruel, furious and insolent. When they utter wicked, gross and insolent words to thy face, when they grow angry with thee and abuse thee, what wilt thou think?'

'This is what I will think;' replied Purna, 'these men are certainly good and kind, who do not strike me either with their hands or with stones.'

'But if they strike thee with their hands and with stones, what wilt thou think of them?'

[3] Admirers of Buddhism claim that it has *never* been spread by force. But it is difficult to distinguish between King Asoka's edicts to abolish sacrifice and establishing religion by force.

'I will think that they are good and kind, as they do not strike me with sticks or with the sword.'

'But if they strike thee with sticks or with the sword, what wilt thou think of them?'

'I will think them good and kind, as they do not take my life.'

'But if they take thy life, what wilt thou think of them?'

'I will think the men of Sronaparanta good and kind, to deliver me with so little pain from this body full of vileness.'

'It is well,' replied Buddha, 'with such perfect patience thou canst live among the Sronaparantas. Go then, O Purna, delivered thyself, deliver others; thyself arrived on the other shore, bring others there; thyself consoled, do thou console; thyself arrived at Nirvàna, teach others the way.'

Purna, thus encouraged, went to dwell among that tribe, and by his gentleness and resignation won them from their savage customs to the law.[4]

Whether this story be true or not, its very conception shows a standard of missionary courage and devotedness that, with all its exaggerations, accounts for the rapid spread of Buddhism through India.

Effects of Buddhism.

The permanent effects of Buddha's life and teaching on India have been very great. He has imbued all Hindus, from the highest

[4] For this, as for most of the incidents here given, I am indebted to St. Hillaire's *Bouddha et sa Religion.*

to the lowest, with a tenderness for animal life. Even the Rajput who delights to hunt and slay the boar looks on the killing of a fly as a sin. We shall see when we come to consider modern Hinduism the great influence which Buddha has exercised on it. But Buddhism has also defects and weaknesses which proved fatal to it in the land of its birth, and which must ultimately prove fatal to it throughout the world.

Defects.

Atheism causes false views of duty,

These defects may all be summed up in one word—Atheism. The absence of God prevents a true conception of duty and of human life. The idea of all that we receive being talents intrusted to us by our Maker, and for the use of which we are accountable to Him, is impossible in Buddhism. The words of King Arthur,—

> 'This life
> I guard as God's high gift from scathe and wrong,'

could never have been uttered by a Buddhist king. Duty as duty and right as right are ignored. They cannot be referred to the will of a righteous Father, but only to their effects in producing an end in itself and of human life.

false. The conception of human life, too, is erroneous. Without God it cannot be looked on as a discipline, but merely as a state of existence, in which as few seeds of future existence as possible should be sown. Loss of life is rather a blessing than a sorrow, and that not because it is the gaining of life eternal, but because it is a step towards final extinction.

Absence of revelation.

Buddha also, by his atheism, shut himself out from the possibility of having any divine revelation; he based his authority only on knowledge, and that knowledge intuitional. He indeed claimed to have arrived at perfect knowledge, and those who became his disciples were required to acknowledge this, but it was an authority which other men could claim to have in an equal degree with him. His religion contrasts in this way most markedly with that of Moses. The Hebrew lawgiver, on the broad basis of a divine revelation and authority, promulgated a religion which offered, in the first instance, only an earthly rest and earthly rewards, and the truth of which every one could test by its fruits. The Indian lawgiver, on the narrow basis of his own intuition and deductions, which every one could test by his own, sought to establish a system of rewards and punishments passing through thousands of millions of ages and thousands of worlds, the evidence of which was beyond the reach of all.

Absence of power consequent on atheism.

But a more important defect consequent on atheism is the absence of all power. Buddhism is a moral system, but it is not a moral power. It offered India a perfect morality without God, but it failed to make India moral, or to secure any hold on it. It offered nothing to satisfy the religious sense in man. Its appeal was to knowledge, not to faith. This want was indeed felt by Buddha's immediate successors, and a canon of sacred literature was compiled by them; legends attributing to him superhuman power gathered round the story of his life. He was represented as the last of twenty-four Buddhas, successive appearances of the same being on earth to teach mankind the way of deliverance. Huge images of him are erected in his temples which quite dwarf all the idols of Hinduism. A system of sacerdotalism and caste was grafted on the simple rules prescribed in his teaching, which makes Buddhism in those lands where it prevails as different from what it originally was, as the Vatican is from the upper chamber in Jerusalem; but nothing has ever been able to fill the original void, or to offer to man's instinct aught to take the place of God, whom it orginally set aside. Buddhism, within a couple of centuries, is said to have spread over all India, but I question whether one idol the less was worshipped in consequence. Even now, in Ceylon, where it is supposed to have had undisputed sway for twenty centuries, it fails to satisfy the religious wants of the people. 'In Ceylon the people look to Buddhism for deliverance as to the future world. By its instrumentality they suppose that they can gain merit; but for present assistance, when the burden of affliction is heavy upon them, their resort is to the demon priest, with his incantations and sacrifices."[5] We cannot suppose that in its rapid spread over India it was anything more satisfying. It was accepted by the people as a protest against priestly pretensions and caste tyranny, but when the test of religion—the hour of trial and affliction—came upon them, they still resorted to the idols and fetishes which they had been wont to worship. A system thus defective and one-sided is smitten with decay; it has foes in its own stronghold, with which an enemy has only to unite in order to accomplish its overthrow.

Fall of Buddhism.

This was what took place with Buddhism in India. In two or three centuries it was triumphant throughout the peninsula, while Brahmanism was confined to the small kingdom of Kanauj on the Ganges.[6] But a struggle then began, which continued till the twelfth century, and resulted in the complete expulsion of Buddhism and the establishment of Hinduism throughout India.

Jains.

The only relic of Buddhism which now

[5] Hardy, *Legends and Theories of the Buddhists*, L. (50).
[6] Marshman's *History of India*, vol. i. p. 11.

remains there is the sect of the Jains, whose faith is in many respects different, but has evidently sprung from that of Buddha.[7]

Founders of Jainism. Pàrswanàth.

The original founder of the sect was Parswa, or Pàrswanàth, as he was afterwards called. He was the son of King Aswasena, and of one of the noblest royal families in India. He became an ascetic when he was thirty years old, and died about the age of a hundred, on Sikhar, a mountain in Southern Behar. Two hundred and fifty years after

Mahàvira.

him, according to Jain chronology, Mahàvira was born of the same stem. He became an ascetic at the age of twenty-eight, and died when he was about seventy-two. The chief difference between him and Pàr-

[7] The Jains indeed maintain that they are older than the Buddhists, and that their founder Mahàvira was the teacher of Buddha. They fix his death about 570 B.C., or about thirty years before the usually accepted date of the death of Buddha. Some European scholars, such as Colebrooke and Stevenson, are inclined to agree with this, while others, such as Benfey, make the origin of this sect to have been about the tenth century after Christ; but this again is obviously too late, as we have evidence of a distinction between Buddhists and Jains as early as the fifth century. Lassen (*Indische Alterthumskunde,* iv. 763), while inclined to fix the date about the first or second century, allows that we must wait further light on the subject before it can be decided.

swanàth was, that while the latter always wore one garment, Mahàvira carried his mortification of the body further, and dispensed with every sort of covering. Hence the two divisions of the Jains have sprung up, the Swetambras, clothed in white, and the Digambras, clothed in space. The latter, however, while still the stricter sect, do not carry out their principles with regard to dress.

Jain doctrine. Twenty-four sages.

These two are said to be the last of the twenty-four Jinas or Tirthankaras,[8] who constitute the chief object of Jain-worship. The preceding twenty-two are evidently fictions, but in the first of them, Rikhab Deva, we have some trace of real historic tradition. Like the Buddhists, the Jains are atheists. They believe in the eternity of the universe both of matter and of mind, —the latter including the elements of human souls—which has been undergoing a series of revolutions produced by the inherent powers

Atheism.

[8] Jina means conqueror, one who has triumphed over the passions. This was also a name of Buddha. Tirthankara means the 'author of a *tirth*,' or place of pilgrimage, visiting which confers salvation. But 'the Jain *tirth* is a moral *tirth*.'

of nature without the intervention of any eternal Deity, no such being, according to them, existing independent of the world. Certain of the world's elements may be sublimated into gods, who inhabit the various heavens that exist, but they are inferior to the Tirthankaras, and must again enter the various hells, or become animals and men as they have been before, till they finally triumph over matter, and can exist free from its trammels. This has by meditation been attained by the twenty-four Tirthankaras, and through their merit by several thousand disciples who were on earth when they attained beatitude. This is the only way in which, according to the Jain religion, final beatitude can be attained, and they themselves acknowledge that the way of salvation is thus limited to very few. In their cosmical system they are nearer the Hindus, while they agree with the Buddhists in their moral code,[9] and in the

Final bliss.

[9] This consists in enjoining five duties and forbidding five sins. The duties are—1st, Mercy to all animated beings; 2nd, almsgiving; 3rd, venerating the sages while living and

extreme respect which they pay to animal and even insect life. They have even in some cities erected and endowed hospitals for diseased animals.

Origin of the sect.

There is little doubt that this religion resulted from the influence of Buddhist and Brahmanical teaching on the minds of those who founded it, though I cannot see that there is any reason for supposing that it is the result of a compromise. In the earlier Jain books the Brahmans are spoken of with great contempt and bitterness. In the Kalpa Sutra, the history of Mahàvira, that Tirthankara is represented as having been conceived in the womb of a Brahman woman; whereupon Indra, the chief of the gods, is represented as reflecting, 'Surely such a thing as this has never happened in past, happens not in present, nor will happen in future times, that an Arhat, a Chakravarti, a Baladeva, or a Vasudeva, should be born in a low caste family, a servile family, a degraded

worshipping their images when deceased; 4th, confession of faults; 5th, religious fasting.

The sins are—1st, Killing; 2nd, lying; 3rd, stealing; 4th, adultery; 5th, worldly-mindedness.

family, a poor family, a mean family, a beggar's family, or a Brahman's family.' He is accordingly represented as sending a messenger to remove him to the womb of a woman of the royal caste. Now, however, the Brahmans seem to have regained their authority among the Jains. Some of the Swetambras are even glad to have them as priests in their temples. At one time Jainism had spread extensively through India, but its adherents are now numerically small, though still commanding a great part of the wealth of the country. They now exercise no influence on Hinduism, and indeed practically have come in faith and practice to differ little from it. By a recent decision of the Bombay High Court it has been ruled that the laws of the orthodox Hindus are binding on the Jains.

PART II.

HINDUISM.

HINDUISM.

Rise of Hinduism.

BUDDHISM seems to have culminated in India about the beginning of our era. Two hundred years before that time it assumed a character decidedly hostile to Brahmanism. At first, though utterly opposed in principle to its claims, it seems to have existed alongside of it on a basis of mutual toleration. But the decrees of King Asoka, a convert to Buddhism and paramount sovereign of India, showed an intention to make the new faith universal in India, to the destruction of the older one. This stirred up the Brahmans to do more earnest battle for their religion, quickened their intellectual life, and made them more pliable in adapting their system to the religious ideas of the various tribes and castes with whom they came in contact. This Brahmanical revival continued to struggle with Buddhism, and by the twelfth century of our era had extirpated it from India. It is to it that modern Hinduism owes its character; and it is, therefore, of more practical interest, and more deserving the study of those who wish to know the religious condition of the millions of our fellow-subjects whom it has influenced, than any form of religious thought that preceded it.

Difficulties of the subject.

The brief survey we have taken of the earlier religions of India, while leaving many questions still unanswered, will yet prepare us for better understanding that complex and subtle system with which Christianity has now to contend. I will not touch on the political movements which aided it, or the warriors and kings who established it by force of arms, but will rather seek to indicate those principles and methods, still in operation, by which it triumphed over its great foe, and attached to itself, or is still attaching to itself, the various races of India. I must now ask the English reader to follow me into a somewhat abstruse and difficult field; to enter a region and method of thought most likely quite foreign to him, but which it is necessary to master to some extent in order to understand Hindu idolatry. To try to explain this on the basis of English ideas, is about as hopeful as trying to explain Indian jugglery on the basis of English regimental drill. I can only promise to endeavour to make the subject as clear as it is capable of being made to persons accustomed to entirely other modes of thought.

Two features of Hinduism.

There are two distinct features in the Brahmanical revival which must be understood in order to grasp the present character of Hinduism,—the intellectual revival among the Brahmans, producing Hindu philosophy, and the application of that philosophy to the popular superstitions, producing the Hindu religion.

CHAPTER I.

HINDU PHILOSOPHY.

Cause of the intellectual revival.

THE first step in the establishment of modern Hinduism was the revival of intellectual activity among the Brahmans. Appeal to the authority of the Vedas was now of no use to them. Their Buddhist adversaries required them to prove all things. They therefore strove to combat them with their own weapons, and in succession rose the six schools of Hindu philosophy.[1] These all started with the professed acknowledgment of the Vedas as the rule of faith, but except one (which, strangely enough, while ignoring God, made the eternity of the Word its fundamental principle), they all practically ignore the Vedas, and found their systems on the deductions of pure reason. The Vedas are now, for the majority of the Hindus, only the

[1] See Appendix B, Schools of Hindu Philosophy.

shadow of a name; so that in this respect Buddhism has practically remained victor, while it again, by accepting a sacred canon of its own, may be said to have been vanquished by Brahmanism,—a fact which its opponents have not been slow to point out. I do not propose to give any account of these various systems, or of the dialectics by which they are supported, but will seek to exhibit their effect in moulding Hindu thought to the form in which we actually find it.

To understand any philosophy or religion aright, we must know what it teaches to be the highest good. Ask a Hindu what is the chief end of man's existence? and he will answer, Liberation.[2] This is the answer which will be given alike by the peasant and the philosopher of any one of the schools. Ask him what he means by Liberation? and he will say that it is 'to cut short the eighty-four.'[3] Here we are already in a sphere of thought and expression quite foreign to the European, and requiring explanation.

The chief end of man.

The Hindus, then, believe man's spirit to

Liberation.

[2] Mukti. [3] Chaurassi Katna.

be a part of the Divine Spirit, an emanation from it which must return to it again. Meanwhile it is in bondage from its union with the body or with matter, and the great aim of man should be to free his spirit from this union, so that it may again be at liberty to join the Supreme. Or as the Hindus say: Man and God are one; but man, owing to ignorance and delusion, cannot now recognise this identity; his chief aim should, therefore, be liberation from this ignorance and delusion, so as to recognise his oneness with God. Such is the briefest possible statement of what is meant by liberation, but I must dwell on it more in detail.

Fundamental principles, *ex nihilo nihil fit.*

The fundamental principle of Hindu philosophy is, that out of nothing nothing can be made; hence whatever now exists must be accounted for by what has previously existed, and therefore our spirits must have existed before. Another principle now almost universally adopted is that of the great Unity;[4] that

Only one existent Being.

there is only one really existent Being, who is from everlasting to everlasting—the Supreme

[4] Ekamevàdwitiyam, one only, without a second.

Lord,[5] or Supreme Spirit.[6] He alone is, everything else is not. Our spirits must, therefore, be part of Him. Such is the argument of the Vedantic, the most influential school of modern Hindu philosophy.

The Supreme Spirit unconditioned.

Now the question comes, Who or what is this Supreme Spirit? It has often been objected to the Vedantic Deity, that it is a mere abstraction and negation, and that therefore the system is atheistic as much as Buddhism. This is founded on the word always used in characterizing the Supreme, which in popular language means void of qualities. But the word means primarily without bonds or unfettered, and this is rather the sense in which it is used in Hindu philosophy. Man's spirit is fettered by union with the body, but not so the Supreme Spirit. He is free. The word which in modern European philosophy corresponds most nearly with it is Unconditioned. Those who are not familiar with philosophical expressions may form some idea of what that means, by trying to conceive the existence of God before anything was created. This is

[5] Parameshwara. [6] Paramâtman.

the point which Ballantyne maintains Brahmanical philosophers have grasped with a far clearer and firmer hold than English or even German thinkers,—the distinction between the Unconditioned[7] and the Conditioned.[8] Now what do the former declare Unconditioned Spirit to be? They say that it is Being, Thought, and Joy.[9]

The Vedantic Trinity.

We, trained alike by the testimony of our own consciousness and by the teaching of the Bible to believe in the personality of God, and to think of Him as distinct from ourselves, have difficulty in conceiving an impersonal God, and in perceiving the full bearing of the above definition. But let us try to introduce into it the idea of personality and consequent relationship, and chiefly the relationship of the Creator to the creature, imparting what He Himself has; and we have: the imparter of Being—the Creator; the imparter of Thought—the Word; the imparter of Joy—the Comforter. Here, then, we have in the Vedantic Trinity a certain

Analogy with the Christian Trinity.

[7] Nirgun. [8] Sagun.

[9] Sat, Chit, Anand, Sachchidananda.

analogy to the Christian Trinity. How this may have arisen we cannot now determine. We cannot say what interchanges of thought may have taken place in the earlier ages of the world. Long before this idea of the Supreme Spirit had been formulated by Hindu philosophy, the germs of the idea of a Trinity had been introduced into Grecian philosophy, and may have been carried into India in the intercourse which the Greeks kept up with it in the second and third centuries before our era. There was also constant communication between Egypt and India at the time when the Judæo-Grecian school of philosophy flourished at Alexandria, ere the Vedanta school rose in India. But I refrain from entering on the field of investigation thus opened up, merely noting the fact, however it may be accounted for and whatever may be its value, that such is the Hindu idea of the Supreme Spirit, and that on this prime question of theology the distinction between Christianity and Hinduism is as to the personality of God.

Man's spirit and matter.

But in maintaining that the human spirit is part of the Divine Spirit, the Hindu is met by those facts which for the Englishman at once decide the question, and against which the whole of Hindu philosophy is a vain struggle,—the facts of consciousness. We are not conscious that we are parts of the Supreme Spirit; we are conscious of limitation and imperfection contradictory of our idea of God. These facts the Hindus too acknowledge; but 'so much the worse for the facts;' they are the effects of *Màyà*. And what is Maya? This it is very difficult to explain. It means properly illusion or delusion. It is an attempt to explain the consciousness of man and the existence of an external world, in accordance with the sole existence of God and the principle,—nothing from nothing. They say that the visible universe is a projection of the spirit, as the shadow is the projection of the pillar, or the figure on the screen the projection of the picture in the magic lantern. They attribute to it two effects,—enveloping the soul, which gives rise to the conceit of personality, and projecting the appearance of a world, which the individual imagines to be external to himself. Spirit

Màyà, or delusion.

thus invested or deluded is what the universe consists of.

Analogy of dream-land.

This abstract speculation will be better understood by means of a simile which the Hindus often employ. They say that the world is just like a dream. We fall asleep; we imagine things to be about us which are only the creations of the brain, but which have for us all the value of realities; we wake up and find that they are all a delusion. So shall we one day wake up and find that all the external universe, which we now imagine to be about us, has been but the play of our spirit, and has vanished 'like the baseless fabric of a vision.'

Analogy from monomania.

A pundit, who had some acquaintance with English literature, quoted to me the following incident, which I had previously read, as a proof of the truth of the Hindu theory:—'A man was once labouring under the influence of a mania that he was so enormously swollen that he could not pass through an ordinary door. Some of his friends tried to persuade him that he was quite able to do so, but he listened to them very much as if they had been trying to persuade him to go through the key-hole. At last they thought the best way to convince him he was wrong was to pull him through, and this they did, notwithstanding his struggles and screams. When he had been got through in this way, he fell down in an agony, as if he had been bruised all over, and died from the effects on his mind.' The door evidently did not appear the same to him as to his friends; but what right have we to explain it by his madness? The Hindus maintain that it is all delusion, and the practical effect on the unfortunate madman showed that his delusion was real enough for him.

Nature of the illusion.

Meanwhile spirit is under the influence of this Maya or illusion, and it is therefore subject to conditions or qualities.[10] As to what these conditions are, they fall back for explanation on an earlier philosophy,—the Sankhya, which accounted for the creation of the world by an eternal *Prakriti*, which modern European philosophers would probably translate by cosmic vapour. It in fact means matter, but the Vedantists have

[10] Gun.

discovered it to be really a delusion, though practically a reality. It is supposed to consist of an equipose of three conditions or qualities,—intelligence, passion, and darkness or indifference.[11] Where intelligence prevails, we have such beings as men; where passion or foulness prevails, such beings as the lower animals; and where darkness or indifference prevails, such beings as trees and stones. The Spirit or Self,[12] imprisoned in all these, is the same with the Supreme Spirit, and the final end of it is to be freed from all, and identified with its parent source. After this liberation, man must consciously strive. Thus the Hindus, groping after the same truth as that expressed by Paul, 'The whole *creation* groaneth and travaileth in pain together until now,' have changed it into, 'The whole *Creator* groaneth and travaileth in pain together until now, waiting for the liberation, to wit, *redemption from* the body.'

Difficulties to be explained.

It might seem at first that at the time of death, when the spirit quits the body, it will be free to join the Supreme. But call it by

[11] Sat, Raj, Tamas. [12] Atman.

what names they chose, illusion or eternal matter, the same problems of the world—joy and sorrow unequally meted, vice prosperous and virtue oppressed—faced the Brahmanical philosophers which faced Buddha, and for them they could give no better solution than he,—the transmigration of the soul. They indeed argue for this partly on the same grounds that Plato does, namely, that all knowledge is reminiscence, and that what we call instinct in a child, leading it, for instance, to take its mother's milk, is but a recollection of what it has learned in a previous existence. But the great argument is the moral one, that we are moral and responsible beings. We commit deeds which merit reward or punishment; happiness and misery in this life are not proportioned to the good and evil deeds of each individual. We see babes, who have done neither good nor evil in this life, born some to plenty and some to poverty; some surrounded with every temptation to sin, and with an inherent proclivity towards evil, others surrounded with every influence for good, and with a natural leaning to virtue

Metempsychosis proved by reminiscence,

and moral necessity.

and uprightness. Hence they conclude that there must be another life, in which present inequalities are redressed, and a past life, by which present inequalities have been caused.

Vicarious atonement.

The idea of vicarious atonement has in one form or another found a place in nearly all systems of religion, certainly in all earlier systems. The instinctive feeling of man, that sin places him in opposition to God and must be punished, found refuge first of all in sacrifice, in which, as we have seen, the principle of vicarious atonement had a place. But this left many of the mysteries of Providence unexplained; how, for instance, sufferings that could apparently not be traced to any cause were to be accounted for, how sacrifice might be attained by some and not by others. This the Hindus account for by saying that men are now reaping the fruit of what they themselves have done, in a previous life, though from the effects of *maya* they are ignorant of it. They thus try to reconcile the principle of natural justice—that every one should suffer for his own deeds—with the principle of vicarious atonement, which seems man's instinctive refuge from the mysterious inequalities and consciousness of sin in the present life. We suffer for what we ourselves have done, but the deeds for which we suffer are deeds which we are not conscious of having done. We are not recompensed for what we are doing now, but we shall be recompensed in a future birth. This brings us to the second bond of the spirit, according to Hindu philosophy, that which binds it within its first bond, the chain which prevents its escaping the prison-house of illusion—Deeds.[13]

Deeds bonds of the spirit. A pundit with whom I had once occasion to discuss the subject used the following illustration: 'We are bound to our existence,' he said, 'by two chains, the one a golden chain and the other an iron chain. The golden chain is virtue and the iron chain is vice. We perform virtuous actions, and we must exist in order to receive their reward; we perform vicious actions, and we must exist in order to receive their punishment.

[13] Karma.

The golden chain is pleasanter than the iron one, but both are fetters, and from both should we seek to free our spirit.' This comparison is a good illustration both of the principles and of the spirit of Hinduism. All action, whether good or bad, binds us, and there is an aim to be sought beyond happiness. If a man of low rank discharges his duty aright, he may in his next birth be a king. If a king rules well, and especially uses his power in the promotion of religion, he may in his next state be born in heaven, and spend thousands of ages there. That might be a state to be desired if there were any certainty of its permanence, but in it he may at any moment commit a slip, or he may unconsciously, in a previous birth, have been guilty of a sin still unexpiated, which will require his being born again in the form of a demon, an animal, or one of the lower castes. There is no security of rest till the spirit is delivered from the idea of its own personality.

Analogy of vapour.

The Hindus try to explain this to themselves by another simile, and with them a simile has all the force of an argument.[14] They say: Spirit is one as water is one; but some water may be drawn up from the ocean in the form of vapour; then it may become a cloud; then fall on the earth in the form of rain; be absorbed by some plant and become its sap, be exhaled from it again to be absorbed in another, and so on, changing from form to form, till at last it may fall into some river and find its way to the ocean. In this figure the ocean will represent the Supreme, Free Spirit, and the other conditions of water, spirit in connection with matter or illusion. When any portion of the Supreme Spirit is as it were exhaled and comes under the power of illusion, it must pass through men and animals, through gods and devils, through trees and rivers, and even stones,—always when it quits one body, being forced by the deeds which it may have committed in that, or in some previous body, to enter another, in order to receive their recompense. So it must continue its devious path, ignorant of whence

[14] See Appendix C, Hindu Logic.

it has come and whither it is going, till the full tale of appointed births, said to be eighty-four lakhs, or eighty-four hundred thousand, is completed. Then its good and evil deeds may be fully atoned for by its joys and sorrows, the spirit may regain its origin, be emancipated from matter, and free to rejoin the Supreme. But the Hindus have also a vague hope that they may not need to endure all this; that they may find a clue out of this interminable labyrinth of births; that they may find a direct passage as it were to the Supreme, and be freed from the necessity of being again born either for joy or for sorrow. This is what they mean when they say that 'Liberation is to cut short the eighty-four.'

The eighty-four.

Thus far the Hindu system has developed itself with a certain logic. But two testing questions naturally occur here—What led any portion of spirit to come under the power of illusion? and, According to what law do these transmigrations take place?

Difficulties.

To the first of these questions the Hindus give some such answer as this: The

Origin of illusion.

Supreme Spirit was one, and he thought, 'I will become many.' There is here a certain recognition of supreme will, but if asked again what led him to wish to become many, they are silent, and allow that there is something there for which they cannot account.

The law of transmigration.

The second question,—What is the principle which requires certain deeds to be followed by certain births? what is the power that binds spirit by the bond of deeds to ignorance and illusion?—is a question which Hindu philosophy has felt the need of facing, but for which it has only one answer—the Unseen.[15] Here too, when it has with its terrible logic worked out its system to the

The Unseen.

[15] Adrishta. Even God is powerless in presence of *Adrishta*, according to this philosophy. 'God being dependent creates this world of inequalities. If you ask on what is He dependent? we reply, He is dependent on Merit and Demerit. That there should be an unequal creation of the merit and demerit of the souls created is no fault of God. God is to be looked upon as the rain. As the rain is the common cause of the production of the rice and wheat, but of their specific distinctions as rice and wheat the causes are the varying powers of their respective seeds; so is God the common cause in the production of men, gods and others, but of the distinctions between gods, men and others, the causes are the varying works inherent in the varying souls.'—Sankaracharya, quoted in Bannerjea's *Hindu Philosophy*.

crushing of all moral principle and all human instinct, it must confess itself baffled. When it has climbed to its most exalted height, from which it can look down on good and evil as inferior accidents, even here it is constrained, like the early Vedic poets, to erect an altar 'To the unknown God.'

Way of liberation.

And how is liberation to be obtained? How are these eighty-four hundred thousand births to be cut short? It might seem that as there was a power beyond their ken, which ultimately ordered all, it would be wiser for the philosophers to confess their own inability to discover what it had ordained as the final mode of escape. But the Brahmans have here a better foundation to go on than the Buddhists—they profess to believe in a revelation, however inconsistently, and however little their method may be found in the books which they receive as inspired. But the answer which Hindu philosophy gives is practically the same as that given by Buddhism. Liberation is not to be attained by virtuous life or by works of any kind. Bad works require to be punished and good ones to be rewarded. We must seek a higher end—deliverance from pain and pleasure alike—and look for it by nobler means, by being free from works altogether.

Knowledge.

Knowledge [16] is the instrument, meditation [17] the means, by which our spirit is to be freed. To avoid all contact with the world, to avoid distraction, to avoid works, and to meditate on the identity of the internal with the external spirit till their oneness be realised, is the 'way of salvation' prescribed by the higher Hinduism. The following are the words of one of their principal authorities:[18]—'The recluse, pondering the teacher's words, "Thou art the Supreme Being," and receiving the text of the Vedas, "I am God," having thus in three several ways—by the teacher's precept, by the Word of God, by his own contemplation—persuaded himself "I am God," obtains liberation.' This is the Hindu philosophical answer to the question, 'What must I do to be saved?' It is called the 'way of knowledge,'[19] and is said

[16] Gyàn. [17] Dhyan.

[18] Sankaracharya.—Bannerjea's *Hindu Philosophy.*

[19] Gyàn Màrg—Knowledge way.

to be the highest and only infallible way; the other ways, at which we shall have to look, being supposed to conduce to it.

Hindu philosophy and Buddhism.

Such is a brief outline—little more, in fact, than an indication—of Hindu philosophy, yet sufficiently full to enable us to understand how it has affected Hindu society and Hindu religion. It will be seen that, in many of its aspects, it differs but little from Buddhism. It may indeed be called a pantheistic protest against it. It is an attempt to supply the void which the absence of all idea of God occasioned in the rival system. It thus supplies a solution of man's problem more agreeable to human nature than Buddhism does. It is pleasanter to think of the inner *I* as eternally existent, coming from the Supreme Spirit and destined to return to It again, than to think of it as destined to ultimate annihilation. It also supplies after a fashion a basis for worship, as we shall see by and by, and thus helps to fulfil a craving of man's soul. But it shows how nearly pantheism and atheism, the 'all god' and the 'no god,' meet. The immortality of

Hinduism differs but little from the annihilation of Buddhism, for it is an annihilation of that individuality and self-consciousness apart from which man can hardly conceive of his own existence. Yet it enables the Brahmans to charge the Buddhists with atheism, and to call their own system theistic as opposed to it. In other respects—especially the doctrine of transmigration of souls, the way of knowledge, the employment of meditation—it is liker a rival than an antagonist.

Causes of its triumph.

Had the Brahmans, in carrying out their principles, been as consistent as the Buddhists, it is probable that they too would have perished from Hindustan, as at one time seemed not unlikely. So long as they confined themselves to abstract teaching, the Brahmanical power made no progress. At last they united it with the popular superstitions, and rallied the various tribes of India around them, though to this day there are some which have escaped their influence, and which they are now seeking to attach to themselves.

It will be seen that the system which I

Hindu philosophy and Christianity.

have tried to describe is not very far removed from many European pantheistic systems, though possibly it is more consistently logical than they are. It will be seen also that, in its ultimate principles, there are two points on which it joins issue with Christianity—one metaphysical and the other ethical.

Metaphysical difference.

The metaphysical difference is that Hinduism teaches the impersonality, while Christianity teaches the personality of God. The

Ethical difference.

ethical difference consequent on the former is, that while Christianity makes good an essential, Hinduism makes it an accident, classing it along with evil as a bond to the spirit. These seem to me to be the two great antagonistic principles of the two systems in their most philosophical aspects; and if we examine their practical developments, we shall find this antagonism only more clearly brought out. And as, after all, practical results are the best test of any system, an examination of the practical popular developments of Hinduism will be the most conclusive demonstration of the falsity of its higher doctrines. Let us, then.

look at the effects which they have on the society and the popular religion of the Hindus.

Popular philosophy.

But, before proceeding to this, one question remains to be answered, Is the account I have given of Hindu philosophy a description of the belief of all Hindus, or of the learned only? I have stated it as I have heard it explained by the more learned pundits and read it in their books on the subject, and the reader may imagine all the different stages of acquaintance with and belief in it down to the utmost ignorance. The following tenets I have found held generally by all classes of Hindus.

Transmigration.

The transmigration of souls is universally accepted. Every Hindu that I have met with believes that he has previously inhabited other bodies, and that he must again tenant others after quitting his present one.

Deeds are bonds.

Deeds are looked on as the power binding him to his existence, causing his present condition, and even forcing him to his present action. If I were to translate the word *Karma* by *fate*, instead of *deeds*, it would perhaps be more intelligible. But the European fatalist looks on himself as impelled by a power altogether external to himself, which, while it deprives him of liberty, excuses him at the same time from responsibility. The Hindu looks on himself as impelled by what he himself has previously done, as reaping the fruit of his own deeds, though not deeds of his present consciousness. Thus a dreadful sense of retribution and responsibility is superadded to that of helplessness, making it tenfold more gloomy and terrible. The full force of this can be understood only by one who has seen a Hindu under sentence of death for a heinous crime, and who, to all appeals to his conscience and responsibility, can only reply by a stolid "*Karm.*" His crime and his punishment alike are the fruit of deeds done, he knows not when or where. How can he escape?

Man's spirit part of the Supreme.

Lastly, nearly all Hindus believe more or less that their inner self—that which passes from body to body—is the Deity. When I have asked a Hindu 'Who is God?' the answer I have received about as often as any other, and from peasant as well as priest, is, '*Jo bole*'—he who speaks. It is possible he may never have thought of the meaning of this answer, but it shows how deeply the pantheistic principle has penetrated into Hindu thought, when even the most uneducated define the Deity as that within them which gives them the power of thought and consequent utterance. The same idea is shown by the words used by many castes in performing the last rites for the dead. As the body is borne along to be burned, the bearers and mourners unite in the chant—

> 'Ràm, Ràm sat hai;
> Jo bole gat hai.'

'Ràm Ràm (God) is existent: he who speaks is passed.' This is their creed of immortality. Man perishes, but God is ever existent. The body dies and is burned, but not so 'he who speaks'—he has only passed on another step towards his supreme source. Hence the word *gati*, or passing—the final passing into God—is the popular word for emancipation or salvation.

Failure of the philosophical solution.

But when the question came to be, What were the multitude to do to obtain salvation? the philosophical solution, the 'way of knowledge,' failed altogether. For every one to become a recluse, to abandon the world, and to devote himself to meditation, would have been to destroy the faith, by causing all who received it to perish from the face of the earth. It was, besides, utterly opposed to human nature, and especially opposed to the Brahmanical supremacy, as it involved the sinking of all caste distinctions. The Brahmans, therefore, left the various tribes and castes to seek salvation by their own way, and sought to gain them rather by showing how their various ways practically led to the same result which recluses attained by severest meditation. Thus the various popular gods and demons, idols and fetishes, which the proud twice-born had so long ignored, at last rose up in power to avenge themselves on the Brahmans, by debasing their high creed to the lowest idolatry and to the vilest worship; while, at the same time, the lowest orders of Sudras obtained a recognition and a place in the caste system. This union of pantheism with caste and polytheism we now proceed to consider.

CHAPTER II.

PANTHEISM AND CASTE.

THE great vitality of Hinduism lies in its institution of caste. I have already had occasion to speak of it more than once, but a fuller explanation of its leading principles will be necessary to enable us to understand its nature and power. Caste, then, is an institution to preserve purity of tribe and class by preserving purity of blood. The most obvious way to preserve this is by preventing intermarriage. Accordingly all the castes of India are endogamous—they marry only within themselves, beyond certain degrees of relationship varying in different castes. This might be considered sufficient to secure the desired end, but eating and drinking also affects the blood. Members of one caste must not, therefore, eat or drink with those of another—must not Meaning of caste.

eat food that has been cooked or touched by them; and some even go so far as to believe their food polluted if one of another caste comes near it while it is being cooked. Some of the lower castes are considered so unclean that contact with their shadows is regarded as pollution by the higher castes. It is no uncleanness, however, for those of lower castes to come into contact with the higher. All may eat food prepared by Brahmans and drink water from their vessels. Some castes of Brahmans even take wives from the lower castes, in which case the offspring are considered to belong to the mother's family; but Brahmans who do this generally marry one wife of their own caste in order to preserve it.

Occupations.

Besides these rules about eating and drinking, each caste has its peculiar occupation and peculiar customs. Barbers constitute one caste, carpenters another, iron-founders a third, brass-founders a fourth, and so on. Some have indeed a wider range of occupation. Brahmans may be priests or soldiers, beggars or teachers. Rajputs may be farmers or servants as well as soldiers, but there are always some occupations which it is forbidden them to enter on. This community of occupation is thus another bond to bind together members of one caste, and to draw a distinction between them and the rest of society.

Family system.

But the full strength of the caste system cannot be rightly appreciated without taking into account the family system of the Hindus. Its tendency is completely to annihilate individuality. The Hindu child finds himself in a family consisting of grandparents, parents, uncles and aunts, and cousins to the second or third degree. His grandfather, or possibly his grandfather's elder brother, is the head of the family, and when he dies he is succeeded by his younger brother, or the eldest of the second generation. He finds that he has been betrothed ere he could understand anything about it, or when he is seven or eight years old the head of the family chooses a wife for him, and the betrothal takes place with great rejoicings. Among his sisters is one to whom he may not give any present, and who may not wear any ornament. She was betrothed when an infant; her husband died when she was a few years old: she is now a widow, looked on as branded with a curse, and must continue the disgrace and reproach of her family to the day of her death. He hears of nothing but the affairs of his caste; he looks forward to no career but assisting his father and uncles in their trade or profession; and when he gains anything it does not belong to him individually, but is thrown into the common income of the family. When he is seventeen or eighteen he takes his wife to his father's house, and a new branch is added to the family. He performs religious ceremonies at his father's death, others a year after, and at least once thereafter he must perform a pilgrimage to some sacred stream or lake, to burn the *pind*[1] to his father's

[1] A large leaf is bent up into a shape like a boat. This is filled with *ghi*, or clarified butter; a wick is inserted into it, and lighted. The frail bark is then, with certain invocations, set to float on the waters. If the flame continues burning till the *ghi* is exhausted, or till the stream bears it out of sight, it is considered a good omen. If it should be extinguished, then it is considered the spirit is not satisfied, but there has been some failure in the required ceremonies.

manes. As his grandfather, father, and uncles, elder brothers, or father's elder brothers' sons, die—for all these relationships are attended to and distinguished by separate names in India—he floats on to the patriarchate of the family to look after the duties and marriages of the younger members. Thus throughout his whole life there is no room for any play of individuality. His whole course is marked out for him by the lines of inexorable custom; he cannot disentangle himself from family ties, much less break loose from caste fetters.

Pantheistic explanations of caste.

We have already seen how caste may have originated, and we have seen how Buddha sought to overthrow it. He taught, as a consequence of his doctrine of transmigration and final liberation, that all men were equal, and caste, therefore, a sin. But it had struck its roots too deeply into society to be speedily eradicated, and when the Brahmans sought to regain their power, they turned Buddha's own doctrines, or rather their modification of them, into an argument in its favour, and thereby of establishing their own supremacy.

For, they say, just as a man's deeds in his former life may have led to his being born a god or a demon, or an animal, so they have led to his being born a Brahman, a warrior, or a sweeper. There is this disadvantage in having been born a man, that, having freedom of judgment and action, he may leave the duties appropriate to his own caste and discharge those of some other; he may quit the society of his own people and eat and drink with others. But so surely as he acts thus he is involving himself in some miserable birth in the future—he is forging a new link in the iron chain of his existence.

Punishment for caste-breaking.

If a man is born in the highest caste for instance, that of a Brahman, the Hindus believe that it is on account of merit acquired in a previous birth. If a Brahman should quit his appropriate duty—if he should seek to gain his food by manual labour rather than by begging, by merchandise rather than by teaching; if, above all, he should mingle socially, eat, and drink with the lower castes, or teach the sacred books to the outcastes, he is leaving some of his merit not fully rewarded; he must undergo another birth in order to receive its full reward, and, meanwhile, he is committing a sin which will necessitate his being yet again born in some miserable condition, that expiation may be made for it.

Lower castes recognised.

And as it was for themselves, so the Brahmans taught it was for every man. Whatever the condition in which he was born, it had been determined by his previous deeds; he could expiate them only by fulfilling the duties of that condition, but, by fulfilling them aright, he could gain a step towards future bliss as surely as the Brahmans. Thus the Brahmans no longer ignored the Sudras; they recognized them by teaching that they, too, were bound by the same order of things, and that by accepting and obeying that order, they could in future births rise to be their equals or superiors. But one point on which the Brahmans always insisted was that they must be acknowledged as the supreme caste—served, worshipped, and fed as gods on earth. Each tribe or family or trade among the Sudras was glad to accept this condition, and to have its respectability and importance in the social system increased by its being recognized as a distinct caste. Thus they were one after the other attached to the Brahmanical system, and instead of the four old castes, we have now writers, carpenters, iron workers, brass workers, barbers, and others, too numerous to mention; each with its old customs, its rules of eating and drinking, marriage and social intercourse, erected into sacred duties. Many of the lower castes are now much greater sticklers for caste customs and privileges than are the Brahmans.

Subdivisions of the Brahmanical caste.

Two consequences flowed from this—the breaking-up of the Brahmans into various castes, and the disappearance of the two intermediate castes. The Brahmans are now broken up into numerous sub-castes, which refuse to intermarry or eat and drink with one another. Each of these has its separate clients in one of the lower castes, though the distinctive character of some is determined by the places of their origin and their sacrificial duties. It would be vain to attempt here any description of all the distinctions that exist among them, so I merely indicate the principles on which these distinctions proceed.[2] But a more important result of this movement was the disappearance of the warrior and mercantile castes as such. Many of the present mercantile castes do indeed claim to be descendants of the old Vaisyas, and the Rajputs claim to be descendants of the old Kshatriyas or warriors. But the Brahmans refuse this claim, or allow it only where it is politic in them to do so. In Rajputana, where the Rajputs rule, they are acknowledged as the second caste, but in Gujerat they are looked on as inferior to many others. On the other hand, the Kayaths, or writers, who do the principal business in the courts in the North-West Provinces, and who are, therefore, much more useful to the Brahmans there than the

Disappearance of the intermediate castes.

[2] It is difficult to say what constitutes a Brahman. The Pushkara Brahmans are said to be descended from a Mer— one of the aboriginal tribes of India—who was taught the Atharva Veda by a recluse in return for certain services he performed. This would seem as if the possession of a Veda gave the right to Brahmanical distinction.

Rajputs, have obtained a declaration from a Brahmanical college in Benares that they are not ordinary Sudras, but are sprung from the warrior caste.[3] But this does not imply any restoration to those privileges of intercourse with the Brahmans themselves, or to that degree of intermarriage with them that was allowed to the Kshatriyas in the code of Manu. The general state of Hindu society may now be described as being divided into two great castes—the Brahmans or twice-born, who are worshipped as gods, and the once-born, who worship them, and who constitute the great mass of the people.

Power of caste.

Meanwhile, I trust I have exhibited with sufficient clearness how pantheistic doctrine has been allied to caste practice. It may be conceived what an iron hold universal custom, backed up by such doctrine, has on the minds of the people. Accordingly, we find that the Hindus pay much more attention to the law of caste than to the law of conscience. A Brahman may be guilty of theft, adultery, or murder, and he will yet be received without

[3] *Friend of India.*

hesitation by his caste fellows. But let him be guilty of eating and drinking with those of another caste—let forbidden meat cross his lips, even though this be by no fault of his own, but by violence have been forced upon him, and he then becomes an out-caste, with whom it is pollution to eat, drink, or have any dealings. Caste, in some of its features, is fast being obliterated. The distinction of occupations is no longer insisted on with the same rigidity as before, but the rules with regard to intercourse between the various castes are still religiously adhered to over the greater part of India. There are, I suspect, few Hindus who would not shun one of their own caste who had eaten with those of another, much more than they would shun one who had been convicted of a heinous crime.

It was hoped some time ago that railway travelling and the facilities that now exist for visiting Europe would soon put an end to caste; but a system so deeply rooted does not die so quickly or so easily. There did seem not long ago to be a movement against it, Vitality of caste.

but there is now a decided reaction, and caste seems again to be reasserting its superiority. One respectable Babu in Bengal, a pleader in the High Court, who had been trying for some time to fight against caste, and to promote intermarriages, has found the fight too hard, has undergone expiation, and re-entered into caste. The expense of the ceremony was five thousand rupees (£500), and he had to spend a similar amount in erecting a temple of Siva, and feeding the Brahmans.[4] In Bombay a most respectable native judge, whose son had visited England, was asked by the Bombay Government to go to England at public expense, to give evidence before the Indian Finance Committee of the House of Commons. He, however, declined, assigning as a reason the persecution to which he was subjected by the Brahmans for having received his son into his house on his return from England, and his inability to obtain the sanction of his caste-fellows to his visiting that country. He adds—

[4] *Bombay Guardian.*

'I therefore think that it would be a farce for me to appear as a witness, and at the expense of the public, when a considerable and intelligent portion of that public not only disapproves of my doing so, but is sure to persecute me by excommunication, against which no human ingenuity in India has yet devised a remedy, and no law of the land or earthly power can give any protection.'

On this, a native reforming journal—the *Indu Prakash*—has the following remarks, which may give the English reader some idea of the tyranny of caste :—

Native testimony with regard to caste.

'The question is not about going to England, but about an unmanly submission to the vilest and most absurd prejudices of the caste system and Hinduism, which nothing can check and uproot but a spirit of noble independence, rigid moral firmness, and genuine patriotism. The prohibition to go to England is the least of our complaints against the tyranny of caste. Does a Brahman wish to marry his daughter at a mature and properly marriageable age? There comes the tyrant caste, and says "You shall not keep your daughter unmarried beyond the age of eight or ten, unless you choose to incur the penalty of excommunication." Does a man wish to countenance either by deed or by word the marriage of little girls plunged into life-long misery and degrading widowhood? Caste says "No, you will be excommunicated." Does a Brahman wish to dine with a man of another caste? However thick friends they may be of one another, caste says "No, you must not do that or you will be excommunicated." Does a man wish to dispense with any of the unmeaning idolatrous ceremonies with which Native society is hampered? Caste says "No, or you will be excommunicated." Does a man wish to dispense with silk cloth and wear ordinary clothes at the time of meals? Caste says "No, or you will be excommunicated." If a Brahman feels thirsty and has no other water but such as is brought by a Sudra near him, he cannot drink it; for caste forbids it at the pain of excommunication. Why, the tyranny of caste extends from the most trifling to the most important affairs of Hindu life. It cripples the independent action of individuals, sows the seed of bitter discord between the different sections of society, encourages the most abominable practices, and dries up all the springs of that social, moral, and intellectual freedom which alone can secure greatness, whether to individuals or to nations. It has pampered the pride and insolence of the Brahmans, by teaching them to look upon themselves, notwithstanding all their weaknesses, as the favourites of gods, nay, the very gods on earth, who are to keep the lower orders in a state of utter degradation and illiterate servitude. Such is our caste system; so unjustifiable in principle, so unfair in organization, and so baneful in its consequences to the highest interests of the country.'

Effect of caste on the English.

Such is the testimony of a Hindu with regard to caste. One other effect of it I would notice, the gap that it has kept up between the English and the Hindus. Englishmen in this country often reproach their countrymen in India with the antagonism, the enmity, the total want of sympathy that seems to exist between them and the natives. It is a sad fact that such a feeling does exist, but it is the natives who are mainly responsible for it. It is they who have made friendly social intercourse between the rulers and ruled impossible. Governed as they are by the English, owning their sway, and acknowledging that it is a just one, they yet look down on them as unclean. It is the Hindu who looks on himself as polluted by the touch of an Englishman, who will throw away his food as unfit for being eaten if an Englishman comes within a few feet of it while it is being cooked, not the Englishman who looks on himself as polluted by the touch of the Hindu. This has no doubt reacted on the English, and produced in their mind a feeling of dislike and antagonism to the Hindus; but the original blame lies with the latter.

Caste a means of propagandism.

Not only has the system of caste thus riveted Hinduism on the Hindus, but it also gives facilities to the Brahmans for gaining over those of the aborigines who are still outside the pale of Hinduism. Whenever they undertake the conversion of any tribe, the first lesson they teach them is, that they must continue performing the customs of their tribe as sacred duties—as duties to which they are bound by their previous births, attending in addition to those relative duties which are the result of their new position, especially worshipping the holy Brahman and reverencing the holy cow. When these points have been acceded to, they are raised out of the position of out-castes and become part of the Hindu system, enforcing with all the zeal of neophytes the old customs and the new privileges and duties.

The worship of the Cow the Sacrament of Caste.

The worship of the cow the common bond of Hinduism.

I have mentioned as one of the duties imposed on all Hindus the reverencing of the cow. This is in fact the only common bond of union for all castes. It would be difficult, if not impossible, to name anything else that commands the assent of all. Some castes worship one god and some another, some have Brahmans for their priests and some have priests of other castes, but, in whatever they disagree, on one point they agree, and that is in considering the cow a sacred animal, and in looking to the attainment of ceremonial purity through it. It is the sacramental symbol of Hinduism in which sectaries of all shades unite. The formal acknowledging of its sanctity is the act by which an aboriginal tribe is erected into a caste and received within the pale of Hinduism; just as receiving baptism is the act by which any one is received into the Christian Church. The bullock-driver whose clothes have been defiled by contact with a sweeper will rub the polluted part on the nose of his bullock, and thus restore himself to purity. The Brahman who has lost caste may be restored to it by taking the sacred pills composed of the five products of the cow.[5] As far as I have noticed, however, it is only for the conservation of caste and purity that it is thus honoured. The Hindus do not pray to it, or seek temporal and spiritual blessings from it, as they do from their idols.

[5] Viz., milk, curds, butter, urine and dung. Notices sometimes appear in the newspapers of Hindus who have visited this country undergoing purification, of which ceremony partaking a compost of these five elements forms a part!

Origin of cow worship.

The origin and growth of this idea it is difficult to trace. It is probable that even in ante-Vedic times, before the worshippers of fire had separated from the worshippers of Varuna and Indra, a certain reverence was attached to the bull or cow. The Parsees in Bombay preserve a sacred white bull in one of their fire temples, and the whole of Parseedom was lately thrown into consternation by the announcement that its tail had been cut off during the night by some mischievous rascal. This recalls the worship of Apis in Egypt. It is probable that among the Hindus too only one bull or cow was originally regarded as sacred. We can imagine how with a pastoral people it would come to be looked on with a certain degree of sacredness, especially when they also became an agricultural and more civilized people, and used the same animal for drawing the plough and pulling their carts and chariots. In some of the Puranas—the more modern religious books of the Hindus—an ancient legend is referred to, telling how the earth at first gave its products with difficulty,

Legend of Prithu.

and how a certain great king called Prithu, having made a great sage the calf before it—*Scoticè* tulchan—obtained milk from it. This was probably originally a simple allegory to express that the 'rugged all-nourishing earth,' Prithivi, supplied food to those who wrought it, as the cow supplied milk to those who milked it. Ultimately the cow came to be the symbol of the earth, and the bull of religion. But this for a long time did not seem to imply any sacredness in the whole genus. In the Vedas the cow is spoken of as used both for sacrifice and for food, and is praised as the best of all food. In the chapter of Manu's Institutes relating to assault, the cow is classed with other large animals. 'For killing a man (unintentionally) a fine equal to that for theft shall instantly be set—half that amount for large brute animals as for a bull or cow, an elephant, a camel, or a horse.'[6] In the chapter on penance, which is evidenly much later, the cow occupies an intermediate position between man and the other animals,

Manu's laws.

[6] Manu, viii. 296.

and killing[7] it is classed along with adultery and other crimes as a sin of the third degree, to be expiated by a long and heavy penance. In it too we find the five products of the cow prescribed as a means of ceremonial purification.

Growth of cow worship.

When once this start had been made we can easily conceive how the idea grew. The Buddhists might oppose to the reverence which the Brahmans paid to the cow the care which they took of all animals, might ridicule them for their attention to one in particular, and call on them for reasons for their preference. The cow would thus come to be identified with the existence of the Brahmanical religion. At all events, when the Rajputs conquered the Buddhists, the cow was for them the symbol of triumph. In the temples erected to celebrate the victory of Hinduism over Buddhism, a bull is represented as standing on a prostrate Buddha. In later ages, when they again struggled with the Mahommedans and expelled them from Rajputana, the point which the chronicler

[7] Manu, xi. 109.

always notices, when he records the triumphs of a Rajput prince, is that he put a stop to the slaughter of kine. There is no article in their treaties with the British Government on which modern Hindu princes insist more strenuously than that prohibiting the slaughter of kine within their territories. It is a crime on which they now look as much greater than that of murder. About ten years ago the regent of one of the native states, having adjudged a man guilty of this crime, punished him by having him tied to the foot of an elephant and dragged about till he was dead—an act for which he was deprived of the regency by the British Government, but for which he had the sympathy of all good Hindus.

CHAPTER III.

PANTHEISM AND POLYTHEISM.

Place of idol worship in Hinduism.

REVERENCE of the cow is the common characteristic of all Hindu castes, but, as I have said, it is not the object of adoration and worship in the way of seeking temporal or spiritual benefits. The Hindus do not look to it for deliverance from sickness or misfortune, for success in business or for 'cutting through the eighty-four,' for obtaining future happy births or for final deliverance. For these they look to their various gods and idols. Each caste has its own gods, sometimes the same as those of other castes, though perhaps originally different. We have seen that it is probable that, during the supremacy of Buddhism, the people resorted to their various gods and fetishes in those conjunctures of life where they found the atheism of that system insufficient. When the Brahmans tried to reconquer India, they allied their religion with those aboriginal deities, which Buddhism had not availed to overthrow. They thus strengthened their own influence and formed what may be more appropriately termed the Hindu than the Brahmanical religion, as it embraces elements to which all castes of Hindus have contributed.

Apparent contradictions.

We are thus brought face to face with the countless gods of Hinduism—the thirty-three of the Vedas having swelled to thirty-three crores, or three hundred and thirty millions. It may seem at first to be somewhat contradictory to the doctrine of there being one Supreme Spirit, that the worship of so many gods should be admitted, and that, if we are ourselves parts of the Supreme Spirit, we should be required to worship other parts. But pantheism cannot conquer fetichism any more than atheism can, while it does what atheism does not, supplies a philosophic basis for such worship. There is a complete logic running through the various parts of the Hindu system, never indeed formally expressed, in so far as I have known, but indefinitely present to the minds of its votaries —welding it into a consistent whole.

The gods means of mediate emancipation.

The position which these popular deities occupy with regard to the Supreme may be understood by recurring to the image of water which I used to illustrate the theory of transmigration. A drop of water may be far away from the ocean, and it may be impossible for it to return thither directly. Nevertheless, if it fall into a stream, its own existence will, so to speak, be absorbed in that of the stream till it reaches the ocean. So, too, are we by our connection with ignorance and illusion hopelessly far away from the Supreme Spirit. By no effort of our own can we hope to overcome this separation, but these gods are, like the rivers, brought nearer to us. They are themselves under the power of *Maya*—the illusion of the universe—as we ourselves are. Hence they have desires and passions similar to ours. They can be influenced by motives and considerations as we are, can be induced to grant temporal and spiritual blessings, to aid our being introduced into a happy state when we are again born, or, best of all, in certain cases, can grant us mediate liberation, by absorbing us into themselves. We then lose existence except as part of them, the burden of merit or demerit which may attach to us is borne by the deity who may absorb us, and so we shall continue till the final cataclysm, when all shall be absorbed in the universal Brahm. The Hindus thus, quite consistently with their own system, attach themselves to the worship of their inferior deities, while, for the most part, neglecting that of the Supreme.

Pantheistic basis of worship.

We thus see how pantheism supplies a basis for idolatrous worship. Buddhism taught that the gods were subject to the same laws as men, and, having no supreme spirit to which to refer them, forbade their worship altogether, and thus afforded no outlet for a craving of man's nature. Hinduism, admitting the gods to be subject to the same laws as men, yet referring them to the Supreme Spirit, made them mediators leading to It. Their very weaknesses and subjection to laws make worshipping them more reasonable than worshipping It; for they can be influenced by motives while It cannot, and can thus be brought under the power of their worshipper, though he may be weaker than they. This apparent contradiction again the Hindus explain by a simile. One man may be much more powerful than another, inasmuch as he may be richer; but the poor man may go to him at night, and, putting a pistol to his breast, force him to part with some of his riches. So the gods are more powerful than we are; but at the same time we, by certain acts of worship, may bring them under our control, and force them to grant whatever we desire.

Facilities for propagandism.

Such principles as these offered great facilities to the Brahmans for adapting to their own system the various gods and worships, with which they came into contact. When they met any idol that was worshipped by any tribe, they had only to represent it as one of the many streams leading into the ocean of Liberation, needing only to be worshipped in the way in which its devotees had been wont to worship it.

Main divisions of Hinduism.

But there are two great streams in which the current of religious thought has flowed in India since the era of Buddhism, the worship of Vishnu and the worship of Siva, called also Hari and Har. Those who attach themselves to the former are called Vaishnavas; those who attach themselves to the latter are called Saivas, and these two great parties include nearly all the modern Hindu sects. The former are distinguished by a *tilak,* or frontal mark, consisting of three perpendicular lines, the latter by a frontal mark of three horizontal lines. There are also various differences in the time they observe fasts, the shape of their temples, the form of their worship, and so forth, with a mere enumeration of which most who have written about Hindu sects are satisfied.

Leading principle of these divisions, faith and merit.

But such external and superficial distinctions could not account for the bitter antagonism that used to exist between the two sects, as is evident from their old sacred books; and which even now breaks out occasionally between them, notwithstanding the reconciliation that has been made, and the essential quietism of modern Hinduism. One must have seen the kindling eye and quickening breath of a Saiva teacher when encountered by a Vaishnava teacher, the violent fury to which the preaching of the former excited a Vaishnava audience, — exceeding anything which Christian teaching produced,—in order to understand the latent hostility that still exists between the two sects. The cause of this must be looked for in the ideas which they respectively represent. They typify two opposite poles of religious thought which have always been found, and must always be found among men,—the one, the Vaishnava, looking to God as the Author of all good, the other, the Saiva, looking to man, as by his own deeds attaining to the good he desires. The discussion thus corresponds somewhat to that between the upholders of Free Grace and of Works, of Antinomianism and Arminianism in the Christian Church. We know what violent animosities, resulting in war and persecution, have existed between these two parties in Christendom, even when they had a common object of worship, and we need not be surprised that, when in India they were symbolized by distinct gods, a similar hostility should be found.

Limitations of the distinction.

It must not be supposed that the distinction is absolute between the two. On the contrary, the worshippers of each god tried to exalt him and extend his worship by appropriating some of the forms more proper to the other, and thus we find certain traits of Sivism shot through Vishnuism, and *vice versâ*. The range of controversy is also much narrower than in Europe. The extremest upholder of the efficacy of 'works' in India is a more rigid predestinarian than the extremest Calvinist. The firmest Hindu believer in the power of 'faith' looks on it as meriting a recompense from God. Yet these indicate the main principles of the two sects, as will be better understood by a short survey of their historical development.

Purânas.

The sacred books, in which we may trace the progress of these two worships, are called the Purànas, which may be translated 'Antiquities.' They constitute the real sacred literature of the great body of Hindus; they embody their actual religious beliefs, and tell about the gods whom they presently worship; while the Vedas are repeated as incomprehensible incantations in that worship, and the deities they extol are forgotten. The Purànas profess to give an account of the various gods, especially Vishnu or Siva, as they belong to the Vaishnava or Saiva sects. They give an account of the creation of the world,—as being produced from Brahma, which they consider a name of Vishnu or Siva, in the character of creator, and they look forward to its being again absorbed into him at the final cataclysm. They give an account of the various ages of the world's history as they conceive it. We find many old legends embodied in them, and can trace the amalgamation of older objects and modes of worship with Brahmanical gods and Brahmanical worship. I will touch only on the most prominent points contained in them, beginning with the worship of Vishnu.

CHAPTER IV.

VISHṄU WORSHIP.

Vishnuism starts from God's supremacy.

IN Vishnu we find typified that form of religious thought which starts from God, and considers Him as the source of man's strength and salvation,—that type of pantheistic thought which starts with the idea of God pervading all things. The pundits, indeed, derive his name from a root signifying to pervade, but it has with more probability been traced to one meaning to go forth. It may originally have been a name of the sun, and he was at all events first worshipped as the sun-god. We have seen that he was an old Vedic god who assumed some importance during the Brahmanical period; and in him we can trace the continuity of the old Brahmanical religion preserved in modern Hinduism. We find in his worship and legends the influence of many cross currents of religious thought, such as tree and serpent worship and arkite typology, and many adaptations of the faith and worship of the aboriginal races ; but these are blended into a more harmonious whole than in the case of Siva worship.

Abstract conception of Vishnu.

Vishnu is represented as resting in a state of blissful repose on the flood, supported on the great mundane serpent, which raises above him its graceful spreading hood; sometimes it is supposed to be many-headed, and all the heads combine to form one large canopy. Thus reposing he is said to typify the Eternal Spirit, and it is possible that as some such conception the Brahmans originally adored him; but it had too little human sympathy to attract the common people to his worship. He is therefore represented as being occasionally roused out of his slumbers by the solicitations of gods and men, and moved to take interest in the affairs of the world, when something had gone wrong in them. Then he becomes incarnate, or rather, as the Hindu expression means, he takes a descent or *Avatàr*. These avatàrs form the main features of his history, and it is by means of them that his worship is linked to Hinduism.

These *avatàrs* extend to the Divine life on earth the analogy of man's life. Thus we Christians, believing that man is born but once, believe that God has become incarnate once for man's salvation; the Hindus, believing that man is born many times, believe that Vishnu has become incarnate many times. As they believe that the spirit of man may pass through animals also, so they believe that Vishnu has become incarnate in the bodies of animals. This gave the Brahmans great facilities in dealing with the aboriginal tribes whom they tried to gain over, or with the votaries of other worships which they tried to amalgamate with their own. They found one tribe that worshipped the fish, and they taught them that the worship was quite right, but was so only if they recognised the fish as Vishnu, who had become incarnate in it. They found another tribe or caste who worshipped the tortoise; this they said was also an incarnation of the same god; another that worshipped the boar: this too was a form in

His avatàrs analogous to man's transmigrations.

Origin of the fish,

tortoise,

and boar avatàrs.

which Vishnu had taken birth. Each tribe was in this way encouraged to exalt its own peculiar deity, but to recognise in it also a manifestation of the one Supreme Spirit; to continue its own worship, and at the same time to correlate it with that of others. This is, I believe, the most probable explanation of the origin of the accounts of the first three incarnations which are attributed to Vishnu. I have found among the Minas traces of fish and boar worship still existing, and it is probable that, before the influence of Brahmanism spread, such worship was more pronounced. We may look on the stories of these incarnations, then, as first of all attempts to gain over some of the aboriginal tribes, though elaborate myths afterwards grew round them. The story of the fish incarnation has so many points of resemblance with the story of the flood in Genesis, as irresistibly to suggest that it must be a reminiscence of the same event linked with this form of worship.

Fourth and

The fourth descent of Vishnu was as a man-lion, and it had probably an origin similar to the three previous ones, in an attempt to attach the worshippers of an idol of this form. The fifth descent, that of the dwarf, is more important than any of the preceding, for it links the worship of Vishnu with the pre-Buddhistic worship of the Brahmanas, with the worship of the sun, and with a worship in Southern India. The outline of the myth is this:—A king called Bali had by his austerities gained power over the gods, and at last performed a sacrifice so potent that even Indra lost his sovereignty. The gods appealed to Vishnu to help them. He appeared before the king in the form of a dwarf, and asked as a boon as much land as he could cover in three paces. The king granted his request, whereupon the dwarf enlarged his form so as to fill all space; at one step he put his foot on the earth, at the second on the firmament, and at the third on heaven, so that there was no place left for Bali but *patàla* or hell. This myth is a later form of the story of Vishnu's becoming a sacrifice which, we have seen,[1] had its origin in early times, and was probably

fifth avatàrs.

[1] See *ante*, pp. 44, 45.

the earliest conception of his 'Descent.' In this form indeed he appears as the destroyer of sacrifice rather than as a sacrifice itself, but that shows the revolution that had taken place in India with regard to the ideas of sacrifice. In later Hindu literature it is the enemies of the gods who are represented as thus gaining power and threatening their sovereignty, and it was thought more consistent with the divine character for Vishnu to gain his end by deception than by sacrifice—to make the former defeat the efficacy of the latter. The three steps have been variously explained, but the most obvious and probably the original one is the rise, the meridian, and the setting of the sun,[2] while the introduction of the dwarf probably came from some form of worship in Southern India, where it still survives.[3]

[2] Two explanations are given :—'Vishnu strides over this, whatever exists. He plants his step in a threefold manner,—*i.e.* "for a threefold existence, on earth (as fire or Agni), in the atmosphere (as lightning or as wind, Vàyu), and in the sky (as the sun, Surya)," according to Sàkapuni ; or "on the hill where he rises, on the meridian, and on the hill where he sets," according to Aurnavàbha.'—Nirukta, xii. 19 ; *Sanskrit Texts*, iv. 64.

[3] Lassen, *Ind. Alt.* iv. 583.

Sixth avatàr, historical.

With the sixth incarnation we enter on clearly historical ground. We see hero worship being woven into Hinduism, and the desire of the Brahmans to represent the great events of history as the result of the interference of their god. This time Vishnu is said to have come to the earth as Parasu Rama, to extirpate the power of the Kshatriyas and to establish that of the Brahmans.[4] This was not a worship likely to be pleasing to any but the Brahmans, and it was probably not their interest to seek to continue it. At all events few, if any, traces of the worship of Vishnu under this form now exist.

Seventh, Ràma.

The great Kshatriya or warrior hero was Ràma Chandra,[5] who, with his wife Sita and brother Lachman, was represented as the seventh incarnation of Vishnu. Ràma was the type of manly virtues, as Sita of feminine grace and fidelity, among the Hindus. His character, though not altogether free from

[4] See *ante*, p. 50.

[5] On this occasion one half of Vishnu is said to have been embodied in Ràma, one quarter in Sita, and one quarter in Lachman.

blemishes, is one of the best and noblest in history, and it is accordingly to the worship of this incarnation of Vishnu that most reformers among the Vaishnavas, such as Ramanuja and Ramananda, have attached themselves. Under this name he is still worshipped by many powerful sects, such as the Sita Ràms and Ramàwats, or disciples of Ramananda.

Incarnation as Krishna.

But more important than any of these—the great feature in fact of the Brahmanical revival—was the adopting of Krishna as the eighth incarnation of Vishnu. As it shows all the force and all the vice of this movement, I will dwell on it more in detail. I have already had occasion to refer to Krishna, the ally of the Pandavs[6] in the great war recorded in the Mahabhàrat. In the later additions to that poem he is spoken of as a divinity. Traditions about him beyond what are recorded in it were handed down, and were current among the Vaisya and other castes; these, with many exaggerations and accretions, had assumed a definite form, and his

[6] See *ante*, p. 52.

worship had taken firm hold on the popular mind, when the Brahmans begun to manipulate it for their own purposes. According to the general story, he lived in his youth in Brindaban, a beautiful forest on the banks of the Jumna. He was supposed to be the son of Nanda, a cowherd of the district. He was noted in his boyhood for roguery, theft, and falsehood. As he grew up he performed several feats, among others killing a bull by which he was attacked, now the unpardonable sin of Hinduism. He thereafter entered on a course of open, shameless debauchery—the part of his history most often celebrated in story and song. When he had grown up he slew Kansa, king of Mathura, and ruled there for some time; but he was attacked by Jarasandh, the king of Magadh, a relation of Kansa's, and, after a stout resistance, obliged to flee. He led his tribe, the Yadavs, away to the far west of India, and there founded the city and kingdom of Dwarka, by the edge of the ocean. From there he aided the Pandavs, and became one of the most renowned warriors in India—his

Krishna's youth.

whole life being characterized by the greatest licentiousness. He was at last wounded by an arrow, which a Bhil had shot at him by mistake, and died of the wound.

Brahmanical adaptation of the story.

The whole story of Krishna is possibly as great a myth as the story of William Tell is believed by some to be. But, mythical or historical, it had laid as firm a hold on the minds of the Hindus as the story of Tell has on the minds of the Swiss, and had been associated with a belief in the divinity of the hero. We may acquit the Brahmans of having invented it, for it is in many points quite opposed to their general teaching, but they found it too deeply rooted in popular faith for them to tamper with it. They therefore adopted it, supplemented it, and directed their pantheistic philosophy to justifying its most revolting extravagances. Krishna was represented as the eighth incarnation of Vishnu. The object of this incarnation was represented as being the destruction of Kansa, the tyrannical king of Mathura, a worshipper of Siva. Hinduism has never been able to conceive of one incarnation to put away sin once and for ever. Something is constantly going wrong in the course of mundane affairs, and to rectify that a god becomes incarnate, without seemingly having the power to affect future events.

Brahmanical inventions,

To get over the difficulty of Krishna's being born of low caste parents, he was represented as a changeling. His real parents were said to be Vasudeva and Devaki, the former being the rightful owner of the throne of Mathura, but dethroned by Kansa. Vasudeva is a name of Vishnu. The writing of the Bhagavat Purana, the chief authority now for the worship of Krishna, is said to have been prompted by a desire on the part of the author, Boppadeva, to establish the worship of Vasudeva. We must look on these names, therefore, as being entirely mythical, and as meaning simply that the worship of Vishnu had been suppressed by Siva, and that Krishna was raised up to re-establish it. It is now, however, accepted as a substantial fact by the Hindus. Kansa is said to have been warned by a voice from heaven that the child of Devaki would destroy him. When the time of her deliverance approached, she and her husband were by his orders manacled and confined in a tower surrounded with guards, but all in vain. When Krishna was born, the manacles fell off, the guard fell asleep. Vasudeva bore Krishna across the Jumna, whose waters dried up at the touch of Krishna's foot, to the house of Nanda, whose wife had just been delivered of a daughter. He changed the two children, and returned with the female infant to his prison. He and his wife were miraculously bound as before; the guards woke up, and informed Kansa that the child was born. He rushed in to destroy her, but she was carried up to heaven, and escaped.

and explanations.

This story may be taken as a purely Brahmanical invention. In the subsequent parts of the story, Brahmanical influence is seen rather in the mystic explanation given of traditions, which had taken too deep a hold to be forgotten or ignored. Once, when his mother had caught him stealing some cheese, and was about to whip him as he deserved, he is said to have opened his mouth and shown her the illusion of the three worlds therein, whereby she became convinced that everything belonged to him, and that she could not question his right to take the cheese if he liked. The bull he killed—the hardest nut for the Brahmans to crack—is represented as having been a demon sent in that form to destroy him. The part of his life most shocking to the moral sense is the story of his adultery with the gopis, the wives of the herdsmen of Brindaban. In the Bhagavat Purâna—where we have the latest philosophizing on the subject—the story is supposed to be related by a sage called Sukhdeva to a king Parikshit; and when he comes to this passage the king objects that the story is highly immoral. The sage replies: that these gopis were heavenly nymphs, who had come to earth to enjoy the society of God, when He became incarnate; that 'he who moves within the gopis, their husbands, and indeed all embodied beings, is their ruler, who only in sport assumed a body upon earth.' In the popular version of the story, too, the follow-

Justification of sin.

ing verse is quoted, which might almost find a place in a Christian work :—

> 'The rosary vain, and vain to call "Lord! Lord!" by day and night;
> If false the heart, then vain the show; in truth doth God delight.'

This seems a noble sentiment, but as applied in the context it means that, if the heart be right, outward conduct matters nothing, that consequently there was nothing wrong in the conduct of Krishna and the gopis, as he was god, and they looked to nothing but his divinity. This to us sounds like disgusting blasphemy, but it shows what pantheism has done for Hinduism. The pundits allegorize, the common people gloat over the plain narrative. Nothing is more marked than the different ways, in which the best educated pundits and the common people meet an attack as to the character of their god. The former fence, explain away, spiritualize all the indecent stories, till they say they derive edification from them. The latter answer plainly: He had power, why should he not use it to please himself in any way he chose?

Why should we quarrel with the play or pranks of the deity any more than with those of a boy?

Images of Krishna.

This is by far the most popular incarnation of Vishnu, and indeed the most popular god in India. Images of him are more frequent than of any other. These are generally attempts to represent him performing some of his feats, but there are also many adaptations of other images that had become celebrated in certain districts. The best known of these is that of Juggernauth in Orissa. It is a shapeless hideous idol, nothing but a black stump with a head upon it. It was probably an old idol reverenced in that part of the country, and when the worship of Krishna spread, it was adopted as one of his names (Lord of the World) and one of his representations, the difference between it and the others being accounted for by saying that his limbs had dropped off on account of his immorality!

Ninth avatâr.

Since Krishna, a ninth incarnation of Vishnu as Buddha is said to have taken place. This was introduced probably for the purpose of conciliating the Buddhists, and also of ascribing to Vishnu all the great movements that have taken place in India. There is still a sect of Buddha-Vaishnavas, who worship Vishnu under the name of Pandurang, but the worship of Krishna overshadows his; it has still more vitality, and is undergoing fresher developments than any other form of Hinduism. A tenth incarnation is looked for, but meanwhile the sovereignty of Krishna is maintained by repetitions of his incarnation. There is a god of the name of Ram-Deva worshipped by some castes in Rajputana. He seems to have been a Rajput who set himself up for a teacher, and was after death deified by his followers. The Vaishnavas secured his disciples by representing him as an incarnation of Krishna. How often this god has become incarnate it would be indeed difficult to say.

Fresh incarnations of Krishna.

Tenth incarnation, the English.

I have mentioned that a tenth incarnation is looked for, called in the Puranas Kalkin. Who or what this is to be is not very clearly decided. I would merely notice an idea that seems to have some adherents in India, that the English are this tenth incarnation of Vishnu.[7] I once found this expressed in a part of India, where, I believe, no missionary had gone before. When I was remonstrating with some Hindus on their worshipping a being who had been guilty of such acts as Krishna, one man replied very warmly, 'Why, these were but his sports. You English have your sports. You have the railway and the steamboat and the telegraph, and no one blames you. Why should you blame Krishna for sporting in *his* way?'

That this idea is held not merely among the illiterate, the following quotation from a work by a Hindu, a native of Bombay, will show:—

'There are traditions in this land which perhaps none has yet attended to with due concern—that the East will be completely changed by a nation from the West; and the tenth avatàr of Vishnu, a man on a white horse, so current among the prophecies of the sacred Brahmanical writings, must be looked on to typify the advent of the

---

[7] But some consider too that the English are afraid of this tenth avatàr. When vaccination was introduced into the Ajmere district, the report spread that it was a device of the English to discover a new incarnation of Vishnu, who was to have white blood, and who they feared was to extirpate them from India.

English in India. Statesmen vainly look upon the Anglo-Indian empire as an accident, something that will not last long; and, though events like the Mutiny of 1857 frequently give to that expression a significance it can never otherwise bear, the prophecy of the West, "Japheth shall dwell in the tents of Shem," and the prophecy of the East relating to the tenth incarnation of Vishnu, a man on a white horse coming from the West, and destroying everything Brahmanical, render it imperative on us to accept, however reluctantly, that European supremacy in Asia is one of the permanent conditions of the world!'[8]

These are the principal incarnations of this god.[9] It will be seen that he embodies the

[8] *Lights and Shades of the East.* By Framji Bomanji. *Alliance Press*, Bombay. The 'man on a white horse coming from the West' is the popular idea of the tenth incarnation. But it is not so stated in the Puranas. The following is the prophecy as it stands in the Vishnu Purana:—'When the practices taught by the Vedas and the institutes of law shall nearly have ceased, and the close of the Kali age shall be nigh, a portion of that divine being who exists of his own spiritual nature in the character of Brahma, and who is the beginning and the end, and who comprehends all things, shall descend upon earth; he will be born in the family of Vishnuyasas—an eminent Brahman of Sambhalu village—as Kalki, endowed with the eight superhuman faculties. By his irresistible might he will destroy the Mhlechchhas and thieves, and all whose minds are devoted to iniquity. He will then re-establish righteousness upon earth; and the minds of those who live at the end of the Kali age shall be awakened, and shall be as pellucid as crystal.'—*Vish. Pur.* iv. 24.

[9] The Bhagavat enumerates twenty-two, including, besides those mentioned here, sacrifice (see *ante*, p. 45), Rikhabha (p. 83), Prithu (p. 137).

natural tendency to hero worship—that he presents the Hindu conception of 'God in history.' It will be seen that the conception is one of might, not united with moral purity; and that the pantheistic philosophy has justified the wickedness and violence of the god on grounds quite consistent with itself.

I now turn to speak of the worship of this god, but will first say something of Hindu worship in general. It is of two kinds, 'the way of devotion'[10] and the 'way of works,'[11] the former being more specially Vishnu worship and the latter Siva worship, though both are now mingled to a great degree. Those who have learned the higher philosophy try to show that both resolve themselves into the philosophic way of knowledge. Vishnu or Siva, as the Supreme Spirit, is worshipped by invoking him under the name of Ràm or Ràma. This, the pundits say, is an aid to meditation. We are apt to forget God, but, by repeating His name, we are kept in mind of Him.

Forms of worship.

Invocation.

[10] Bhakti Marg. [11] Karma Marg.

Such may have been the original meaning of this worship, but power is generally supposed to exist in the mere sound; and its repetition is supposed to impose an obligation on the god, in return for which he is bound to grant favours, as much as the merchant is bound to give goods in return for the money which he receives. The oftener the name is repeated, the greater the obligation on the part of the god becomes. Sincerity, even purpose and intelligence are not necessary to give efficacy to the invocation. A story is currently told

Story of Valmiki.

of a Bhil, who, having unwittingly killed a Brahman, was told constantly to repeat the word *Marà* (dead) as an expiation. He did so for years, and the transposition of the syllables 'Mara mara' formed the invocation 'Rama, Rama,' till at last Vishnu, hearing himself invoked, appeared to the man, granted him enlightenment, and promised him liberation on condition that he would write a book to promote his worship. The man then became a Brahman, and was known as Valmiki, the author of the Ramayana. Even more absurd stories are told to illustrate the same idea, and it has come to be fixed in the minds of the Hindus that the mere repetition of this name is sufficient. Hence they use it on almost all occasions—the Vaishnavas to invoke Vishnu and the Saivas to invoke Siva.[12] They use it as a salutation on meeting, they use it as an exclamation of wonder. When not otherwise employed, they mechanically turn round their rosary and mutter the name at each bead.

Image worship.

But it is more generally through their images that the gods are worshipped. This brings up the whole question of image worship or the worship of material objects. 'Stone worship' is as common a name in India as image worship, and many of the objects of worship—more however among the Saivas than the Vaishnavas—are mere stones or rocks with a red daub upon them. This form of idolatry does not seem to have belonged originally to Brahmanical worship, but to have been engrafted on it from the worship

[12] The distinctive Vishnu invocation is *Hari Ram*, and the Siva, *Har Ram*.

of the aboriginal tribes or earlier settlers in India. But it now flourishes in it with all the vigour of a stronger life, and the Brahmans have come to be as degraded stone and image worshippers as any.

Three views of image worship:

There are three views with regard to this worship in India. The first is the philosophical, held by the educated and thinking few, that the image is an aid to meditation and devotion. We are apt, they say, to forget God; but when we see the stone it reminds us of Him, we meditate on Him, and invoke His name. But a much more general view is the mystical one, that, according to the charm originally pronounced at the consecration of an idol, indicated by certain red marks on the stone or by the form of the image, some particular deity is present in it. This doctrine is somewhat analogous to the Roman Catholic doctrine of the real presence; but the Hindus do not believe in a corporeal, only in a spiritual presence—that the spirit of the god comes at the bidding of the priest into the idol, as a man might go into a house to dwell, and that he knows and

Philosophical,

Mystical,

accepts what is offered to the idol as offered to himself. And, lastly, there is the literal view, held by the most ignorant of the population, that the idol, by the Brahman's charm, is itself made a god, and by its own power and will can accomplish for its worshippers what they desire. Hence the Hindus, if their prayers are not fulfilled, sometimes scourge their idols or cast them out of their temples. Sometimes the priests exhibit them loaded with chains, and tell their devotees that their god is in debt, and has been put in chains by his creditors, and so must remain till his debts are paid. This is made the means of extracting money from the deluded worshippers. Literal.

I have spoken of the mantras or charms which the Brahmans use in consecrating idols. These are mostly passages from the Vedas, repeated still in their archaic language —a language quite unintelligible to those who use them, as the source whence they are derived is unknown.[13] They are thus nothing Charms.

[13] A pundit, well read in ordinary Sanskrit literature, calling on me one day, happened to look over a volume which I had

better than unmeaning formulæ, but they are supposed to have power over the gods; hence the common saying, that the gods are subject to the mantras, and the mantras are subject to the Brahmans. These last are thus supposed to be able to compel the presence of the god into the image which they wish to consecrate. But many sects hold that each worshipper is able at pleasure to enjoy the presence of his deity, and for this purpose, when he is initiated into the sect, its peculiar mantra or formula is taught him. This generally consists of a short Sanskrit form, meaning 'I salute Krishna,' or 'I salute Narayana,' or some such thing. By repeating this at the commencement of any act of worship, they believe, the presence of the god they invoke is secured, as really as in the idol. The philosophical explanation of this is, that the repetition of the formula helps to concentrate the mind on God, and to enable us to meditate better on Him.

of the Rig Veda with commentary. He was quite startled to find in it certain *mantras* which he had been using for years; to learn that they were in the Veda, and had a meaning.

Disappearance of sacrifice.

One of the most striking facts in modern Hinduism is, that in acts of worship, whether of these idols or of the deity conceived as spiritually present, sacrifice, which formed the centre of early Vedic worship, is conspicuous by its absence. Offerings are indeed made to the idols, but they are not considered expiations for sin. They are looked on as food for the gods; they are allowed to remain before the idol long enough for it to be supposed to have consumed their essence; and then their apparent remnant is taken by the priests. Bloody offerings, sacrifices of goats and buffaloes, are common in many parts of India, as were also sacrifices of children till the British rule was firmly established. But these are acts of fetish worship more akin to the worship of the African tribes than of the early Aryas—different alike in name and in purpose—bloody food offered to propitiate a bloodthirsty deity, instead of symbols of the sins of the sacrificer being borne by another. They are found chiefly among the aboriginal tribes; the tendency of Hinduism is to put them down,[14] and where they have been incorporated into it they form one of its greatest stains. Brahmanical sacrifice has disappeared from Hinduism as completely as Levitical sacrifice has disappeared from Judaism. In the latter it has been fulfilled, in the former it has been superseded. It was impossible that it should continue after the revolution in Indian thought which Buddhism had accomplished. Primitive sacrifice could not consist with the idea of transmigration. Vicarious atonement by sacrifice could have no meaning for persons, who looked for vicarious atonement through another consciousness of their own selves. When the human soul is considered part of the divine spirit, there is no one to whom atonement can be made.

[14] Near Todgurh in Mairwara is a temple to Piplàj or Devi, where the Mairs, an aboriginal tribe, used to sacrifice children, till the district was subdued by the English about the year 1820, and where till within a few years thirty or forty buffaloes were annually sacrificed with the most savage cruelty. A Vaishnava Brahman was appointed Tahsildàr of the place for a few years, and forbade the sacrifice, but under his successor they were renewed. The attention of Government being called to the subject, the sacrifice was allowed, but the cruelties attending it forbidden.

These general remarks on Hindu worship and ceremony will enable us better to understand the peculiarities of Vishnu worship. It suits the character of the god. He is the sovereign source of power, and his worshippers need only to make a formal acknowledgment of this. Their worship is therefore the 'way of devotion.' They go to his temples, and make a presentation of 'wealth, body and soul,'[15] but this with the majority is a mere form; it does not mean renouncing any gain, pleasure or sin. A god who so pampered his own body while on earth, cannot ask anything very severe of his followers—a god who committed such sins as he did, will not require any very strict renouncement of sin from his worshippers. Their main idea seems to be just paying to the idol the same respect as they would pay to the god if he were still incarnate as a prince on earth. The idol takes the place of the king; the temple is his palace. Vishnu worship.

When George I. became King of England, Worship of his images.

[15] Dhan, Tan, Man.

his Court was still kept up in Hanover. His usual levees were held, but in his place a portrait of him was set on the throne, and the courtiers bowed to it as they would to the king. In the same way the Hindus bow to the images of Vishnu—as they would to Rama or Krishna were they still on earth, and they have a better reason for it than these Hanoverians had, for they believe that their god *pervades* the image, and is conscious of service done to it as of service done to himself. They therefore go every morning to his temple to pay their respects to him as they do to their Rajas or Thakurs.[16] In fact, the popular name for an image of Vishnu is Thakurji. They believe that, just as a prince is satisfied with the appearance of his subjects at his court, and as he will grant their petitions, so is the idol satisfied with the presence of his worshippers in his temple, and ready to grant their prayers. So too as a subject, when he wants any great boon from his raja, must make him and his ministers large presents, must they occasionally be

[16] A noble or landed proprietor next in order to a raja.

ready to make large gifts to the idol and to his priests—even to the extent of wealth, body, and soul—especially if they are seeking liberation. Some idols are more specially worshipped on certain days—as kings have greater levees on their birthdays. Then pilgrims throng from all parts of India in crowds; the god is carried out in procession, and exhibited to the attendant multitudes, who are told that a glimpse of it removes all sin. The most famed of these festivals is that of Juggernauth in Orissa, whose identification with Krishna I have already noticed. At it the Hindus make a sacrifice of something dearer to them than wealth, viz., caste, for then all castes mingle promiscuously, and the worship of the god is supposed to sanctify the breaking of caste rules. Formerly devotees used to throw themselves before the wheels of the huge car on which the idol was mounted, to be crushed to death, assured that thereby they would attain union with him.

The Bombay Maharajas.

This consecration of wealth, body, and soul, as worship, produces in some sects still more pernicious results. Some, such as the Maharajas of Bombay, teach that the god is not present in the idol, but incarnate in the priest, and that it is to him that the consecration must be made. As the worshippers throng into the temples, where the Maharajas sit enthroned to receive their homage, guards are stationed at the gates with whips to scourge all who enter, so that they may experience the effects of the anger of the god, and this is considered part of the consecration of the body. In more esoteric worship they emulate the example of their prototype Krishna, and justify their doing so on the same principles as those on which the Puranas justify his conduct. But 'it is a shame even to speak of those things which are done of them'—in worship. When the books of a similar sect—the Bahm Margis—were first discovered by Professor Wilson, he declared that he believed there must be some allegorical meaning attached to them, because no human beings could be found so debased as to practise what was therein inculcated as the worship of God. But, about ten years ago, a trial on an action for slander brought by one of these Maharajas against a native editor, who had exposed him, revealed the practices of the sect in an English court before English judges. It showed that these sacred books were no allegories, that, on the contrary, they did not sufficiently depict the vile licentiousness of the orgies which they sanctified with the name of worship.

Vice a fruit of Hinduism.

And this is only a legitimate deduction from the higher principles of Hinduism. When once Pantheism has shown that virtue and vice are alike indifferent for salvation, and thereby cleared the way for the acceptance of such a character as Krishna as an embodiment of Deity, the way is further cleared for his worshippers seeking to be like him. Happily the power of conscience within even them is not altogether effaced, and the worst of them is better than their deity, while it is only a small section, I would fain trust, that belong to these more degraded sects. Many Vaishnavas walk according to the light of nature, and are exemplary in all the relations of life; but the strange thing is, that when they feel their sin, their need of forgiveness and of the aid of divine power, they should resort to a god capable of appearing in such forms and doing such deeds; and that they should be satisfied with the slight ceremonies imposed by his worship. The Vishnu religion is well termed by the other sects in India the self-indulgent way of salvation.[17]

Vaishnava reformers.

The Vaishnavas have produced many reformers both philosophic and popular.

Ramanuja.

Foremost among these was Ramanuja, who lived early in the twelfth century, to whose influence subsequent reformers owe most of their impulse. He held the theistic doctrine of the personality of God and of His distinction from the universe and from the human soul. He attacked the pantheism of the Vedanta with a dialectic power and high moral tone such as few controversialists have reached. He denounced as blasphemous the doctrine of God's being active only when conditioned by Màyà, or ignorance, and maintained that all the conditions of

[17] Pusht Marg.

sovereignty and activity were eternally God's. But he did not get quite clear of all pantheistic ideas. He maintained that at the final liberation souls were absorbed in God, but not unified with Him. He looked on the union as a mechanical mixture, while the Vedantists would consider it rather a chemical mixture. As milk though mingled with water does not become water, so neither do human souls, though absorbed in the Supreme by virtue of meditation, obtain identity with Him.

One of his successors, Ramananda, modified this, and maintained that the Supreme Spirit might be both unconditioned and conditioned, becoming the latter out of love to his worshippers. The concrete form which this speculation assumed was that God, out of love to man, became incarnate; and the most popular writer of his school, Tulsidas, author of a version of the Ramayana in the vulgar dialect, expresses this in language that a Christian might almost use. The followers of Ramananda, called Ramanandis or Ramàwàts, worship Vishnu in the incarnation of

Ramananda.

Tulsidas.

Rama Chandra. Their philosophical reform was accompanied by a practical reform, which sought, among other things, loosening the distinctions of caste and spreading sacred knowledge in the vernacular instead of the obsolete Sanskrit.

Other reformers.

As they fell from their first zeal other reforming sects sprang from them, some of them emulating in their self-denial the severest of the Saiva sects. But the Nemesis of their origin seems to have followed them all. Starting from the worship of a sensual god, they all sunk to his level. After a protest against religious corruption, which endured for little more than the life of their founder, their worship sank to a grossness emulating that against which they first protested. The latest, and in some respects the most earnest Vaishnava attempt at reform—the Ram Sneh sect, which admits other castes as well as Brahmans to be ministers of religion, and discards all idol-worship—has sunk as low as the lowest, and confounds the practice of uncleanness with the service of God.

CHAPTER V.

SIVA WORSHIP.

Principles of Siva worship.

TURNING to the worship of Siva, the other great god of the Hindus, we find the opposite pole of pantheistic thought at work. Vishnu worship starts from the idea of God condescending to man, Siva worship from the idea of man raising himself to be God. Vishnuism, considering that God pervades everything, has recognised Him especially in the heroes of the nation; Sivaism, considering our souls to be part of God, teaches us to seek to realise that union by subduing the body and mortifying the flesh. We have seen that the idea of the power of austerity entered early into Indian religion, and was by some considered the source of the power of the gods[1] even before the rise of Buddhism; but it was after the rise of that

[1] See *ante*, p. 50.

system that this stream of thought gained power in India, and it was possibly in seeking to combat Buddhism with its own weapons that the Brahmans were led to exalt the worship of Siva.

Rudra. It is difficult to say how he came to take the place he has done in the Hindu pantheon. The meaning of his name is 'Gracious.' The word does not occur in the Vedas as the name of a god, but it occurs as an epithet of Rudra, with whom Siva was afterwards identified. This was the name of the god of the storm, and it explains a number of the attributes of Siva. The storm, rushing down from the mountains, led to the mountain being considered his abode; the constant muttering of the thunder, which the echoes appear to make incessant for hours, might suggest his constant invocations on the mountain top; the irresistible power with which the lightning strikes those on whom it falls might originate the glance from his eye that consumed those who excited his wrath; the destructive fury of the storm, overthrowing houses, tearing up trees, raising the torrents to sweep away their banks, explain his attributes as the god of destruction; the aspect of the plain after the storm has swept over it —the plough turning up the soft earth, formerly a hardened cake—a tinge of verdure clothing what was formerly a barren waste—is sufficient to account for his being called also the god of fertility and reproduction; whilst the effect of the storm in purifying and clearing the atmosphere, and bracing up the frame, may account for the medical power attributed to him.

Popular conception of Siva.

Such is the Vedic god with whom Siva is now identified; and so we may account for some of the attributes now attached to the latter. But this is a more recent identification, and it is probable that, as he is now generally conceived of in India, he was originally the god of some of the aboriginal tribes.[2] The myths about his first forcing Brahma and Vishnu to acknowledge his power—too coarse to be repeated here—

[2] 'Two deities were especially worshipped by the Brahman priests, and appear to have been the types of two different races —the Aryans and the Turanians. These were Vishnu and Siva.'—Wheeler's *Hist. of India*, vol. iii. p. 67.

point to the reluctant acknowledgment of his claims by older sects. There is little human interest in the legends regarding him—nothing, as in the case of Vishnu, to intertwine him with the history of India. The popular idea with regard to him is that he was a mendicant who gained and maintains his power by austerities, meditation, and invocation. In his statues he is represented with his hand open, as if begging for alms: he is said to have gone about begging, riding on a bull, which is consequently now considered his sacred animal. Stories of drunkenness, licentiousness and ferocious cruelty are attributed to him; but his vice differs from that of Krishna's very much as a half idiotic boor's might differ from that of a prince. The conception of a man becoming god through godlike, because most perfectly human, conduct, has no place in Sivaism. The mendicant becomes a terrible god by becoming as un-human as possible, and all the representations of Siva carry out this idea. He is represented as having a third eye in his forehead, with a glance from which he strikes dead

Representations of him.

those who offend him; his rosary is composed of human skulls, in which he is said to delight, and his necklace is of the same; while serpents mingle with his hair and wreathe round his neck. He is said thus to be sitting on Kailas, an unseen mountain of the Himalayas, still engaged in meditation, turning his rosary and engaged in invocation, thereby continually increasing his power. This power is not connected with any moral or even intellectual greatness, or any power of will. It seems to be very little under his own control. One unfortunate god is said once to have disturbed him at his invocations; his anger was aroused, and a glance from his eye reduced him to ashes. When reproached for what he had done, he granted him to be born again as Krishna. So too in a drunken fit he is said once to have struck off the head of his son Ganesha, and when reproached by his wife for so doing, he replaced it with an elephant's head. One name by which he is known among the common people is the simple or half-witted lord.[3] Their idea seems

Saiva legends.

[3] Bhola Nath.

to be that this simplicity makes it easier to cajole, and at the same time more dangerous to disturb him.

Other worship connected with his.

He is said to be married to a goddess named Parvati, which means daughter of the mountain. The *linga* or symbol by which he is now generally worshipped is considered by some to have been adopted from some of the aboriginal tribes, and incorporated with his worship before it was recognized by the Aryan castes. But the main feature in his religion is, that he symbolizes the results that may be attained by austerities and invocation. The very absence of inherent greatness or power in the character of the god tends to exalt the principle which he represents.

The recluses the mainstay of his religion.

In conformity with this, the worship paid to him starts from the idea of getting power over him by similar austerities and meditation. It is therefore called the way of works[4] or the way of hardships.[5] Accordingly it is the ascetics and devotees who form the main strength of the Saiva sects.

[4] Karma Marga.

[5] Kasht Marga.

Some of these include men of real learning and power, who discard all the gross traditions with regard to their god, look on him as the representative of the Supreme Spirit, and endeavour by study and learning to acquire such knowledge as shall enable them to realize their unity with him. Sankaracharya, perhaps the greatest master of the Vedanta philosophy, belonged to the Saivas; its most strenuous and able supporters at present are to be found among them, especially in the sect called the Dandis, among whom alone, as far as I have observed, are iconoclasts and zealous reformers on a purely Hindu basis to be found. These adopt in its highest sense the Saiva principle of man raising himself to unity with the divine.

Common ideas of the meaning of asceticism.

But in general it is a mere mortification of the flesh, a mere unhumanizing of the man, that is looked to as the means of attaining power. A story is told of one who for a thousand years continued standing on the tip of his left toe, during the first hundred years of which period he lived on fruits, the second hundred on withered leaves, the third hundred on water, and the remaining seven hundred on air. At the end of this period Mahadeva, or Siva, appeared to him, and granted him what boons he desired.

Drying up of the blood.

There is a local tradition at Pushkar, near Ajmer, to the effect, that on the occasion of a great gathering of gods and Brahmans at the place, some of the latter went to pay their respects to a celebrated recluse of the name of Mankan. One of them had some coarse grass in his hand, with which he accidentally cut the recluse's finger, when instead of blood a green fluid came out. Seeing the effect which his devotions had had, he began to dance with joy and pride, till Siva, to humble him, went and opened his own finger before him, when a stream of white ashes came out. Mankan, seeing proof of a devotion so much more powerful than his own, became silent, and worshipped him. Then, after asking and obtaining the promise of certain blessings for those who should visit his hermitage on certain days, 'Mankan became absorbed in Siva.'

Practices of modern ascetics.

This story points to an idea held by others as well as Hindu recluses, that the source of corruption is especially in the blood, and that if it can be dried up the passions will be subdued. Among the present ascetics, however, we find little more than a mere symbolism of ancient ideas. They do generally succeed in making themselves appear very unhuman, as unlike men as men can be, though whether it be a sublimation or degradation of their nature depends on the point of view from which they are looked at. The body is covered with ashes, to signify the drying up of the blood, the scorching up of the passions. It is sometimes further mortified by self-inflicted tortures. One arm is held out straight till it is stiffened, and cannot again be bent. The hand is clenched and the nails allowed to grow through the flesh. Occasionally a vow of silence for a period of twelve years is taken. Some live alone in the woods or in caves, but more frequently they wander about from one shrine of Siva's to another. Some classes of these recluses—and there are as many kinds as there are of monks and friars—are more exclusive as to the castes which they admit into their fraternity. But in general men of any caste may join one or other of the various kinds of mendicants, and a short conversation with any of them will reveal the utterly sordid, selfish soul that exists beneath these outer disguises and self-inflicted tortures, symbolizing the mortification of the flesh and its lusts. 'Whose god is their belly' may be said of most of these holy men, and is said of them by the Hindus generally. Many proverbs and rhymes are current among the common people satirizing these *jogis,* as they are called, for their sordid or cowardly motives in becoming recluses, and for their gluttony and rapacity since they assumed their profession. But with all that they fear them, dread their curse, supply them with what they want, and even worship them. They often ask them to obtain favours for them from Siva, believing that in some way their austerities have brought him under obligation to them.

Their degraded character.

These constitute the mainstay of the Saiva

sect.[6] They are the principal worshippers of the god, but they have also a large lay following among various tribes and castes, whose objects of worship they have identified or connected with Siva. The Vaishnavas, we have seen, represented the deified heroes of India as successive incarnations of their god, thus utilizing the doctrine of transmigration. The Saivas, on the other hand, rather took up the primitive objects of worship of the various tribes, and represented them as being either manifestations or servants of Siva. Their system consequently does not present the same unity as that of their rivals; there are no broad lines by which to mark their working, and we have to pick up and put together numbers of disjointed legends in every district of India, to learn how they propagated their faith. In some cases, indeed, their course of action is plain enough. A god or goddess may have more than one name. Thus Devi, who was worshipped by the Rajputs, Màta, a goddess of some of the

Saiva propagandism.

Siva's wives,

[6] In saying this I refer especially to Northern India, to which alone my personal observation has extended.

hill tribes, Durga and Kali, Bengal divinities, were all identified with Pàrvati, the wife of Siva. These were all more or less sanguinary deities, and had thus an affinity with the servants, savage, un-human nature of Siva. Again, the favourite deities of many agricultural castes were Bhairon and Khetrpal. These were allowed to remain and be worshipped as of old, but they were represented as attendants on Siva. The Hindus often say, that if any one wishes to get a hearing of the magistrate, he must tip his servants; and so the farmers think that the best way to secure Siva's protection for their fields is by paying and priests. attention to his subordinates. Another point to be noticed is, that the priests in many of the temples of these deities are not Brahmans, but members of other castes, the former not seeming to have cared to disturb the usual arrangements for worship among those whom they sought to proselytize, if they only acknowledged their supremacy.

Instances of propagandism. But it is only when we begin to examine into the history of each old shrine that we find with what marvellous ingenuity the

Brahmans have made themselves 'all things to all men.' Of this I will give one or two examples, that have come under my own observation in India.

About six miles distant from Ajmer is a lake of the name of Pushkar, with a town of the same name on its banks, considered one of the most holy places in India. As a god may be present in a stone or image, so he may be present in any locality—in a grove, a stream or lake. There are some streams, such as the Ganges, and some lakes, such as Pushkar, which are supposed to be the abodes of powerful deities, who are bound to grant forgiveness of sins to all who may worship them by bathing in their waters. These localities are called by the people tirths, or places of pilgrimage, but by the initiated this name is applied only to the deity who gives sanctity to the place. The lake and town of Pushkar are there throughout the year, but the *tirth* is there for only five days at the beginning of winter. The explanation of this given in the sacred books is: that such multitudes were obtaining salvation by his means, that the gods

Pushkar. Tirths.

complained that heaven was becoming too crowded, and remonstrated with Brahma, who thereupon removed Pushkar to the sky except for these five days. On other occasions he can be drawn into the waters by the use of certain charms. The probable explanation seems to be, that from time immemorial a fair has been held at that time, as being the most convenient time of the year, and the Brahmans afterwards tried to give it a religious reason.

Primitive worship of Pushkar.

In the traditions and rites connected with this lake, we can see different stages of religious thought and worship fossilized, as in the successive strata of a fissure of the earth we find traces of successive developments of life. We see first of all the aboriginal inhabitants with their tree and serpent worship. Then came the Gujars, a pastoral tribe, who worshipped a goddess, Gaitri, and who seem to have been the first, as they are still the most devout, believers in the efficacy of Pushkar. Then came the Brahmans, at a time when Brahma was still their god, and they had not yet found it politic to adopt either

Vishnu or Siva.' They performed a great sacrifice at the time of the fair, which they represented as being a sacrifice performed by Brahma. To symbolize the adherence of the Gujars to their faith, they invented a legend to the effect that Brahma, in the absence of his wife, Savitri, had been obliged to espouse Gaitri, in order to accomplish the sacrifice. They likewise accounted for the serpent worship by representing a Brahman as having been, by the curse of another, changed into a serpent, and having been solaced by Brahma with the assurance that divine honours would be paid him. Pushkar is now the only place in India where the worship of Brahma occupies a conspicuous place.

Saiva manipulation of the legends.

Lastly came the Saivas. They found the legends of Brahma too strongly rooted to be ignored or displaced, so they recast the story, representing Brahma as asking permission of their god to perform the sacrifice, and frequently admitting his supremacy during its course. They also identified Siva with some of the most popular objects of worship in Pushkar and the neighbourhood.

One tradition has been already referred to.[7] The cell of a holy man called Atmat, or the wanderer, had been an object of superstitious reverence. He was introduced into the legend as a servant of Siva, absorbed into him during the sacrifice. The name of Atamteshwar, or Lord of Atmat, was given to Siva, and a handsome Saiva temple erected over the hermit's cell. Again, at a place not far from Pushkar, there is a rock called Ajogand,[8] with a mark on it, said to be that of a goat which, on a certain day of the fair, the people had been accustomed to visit and worship. The Saivas laid hold of this, and represented the goat, whose print was on the rock, as a form into which Siva had transformed himself in order to kill a demon. They also represented him as promising to leave his Himalayan home for one day in the year, and to be present then in that rock—the day of course being that consecrated by popular usage.[9]

Object of Brahmans to assimilate.

It will be seen that the whole object of

[7] See page 190. [8] The leaping goat.

[9] There are Vaishnava traditions also connected with Pushkar, but these are evidently more modern, and refer to historical events.

the Brahmans was to assimilate, not in any way to eradicate, ancient religious usages. They seem to have been as compliant with regard to the moral practices of those whom they thus proselytized. In the 'Lay of Pushkar,' the Gujars are represented as being most loose living men, but their admission as such seems to be looked on rather as an evidence of the catholicity of the Brahmanical religion. As they were then so they are now, after centuries of Brahmanical supremacy.

To the south-east of Ajmer is a district inhabited by a tribe called the Parihar Minas. An incident in the history of one of their progenitors, according to their present tradition, has led them to look on the boar as a sacred animal, though this may be a relic of boar worship. When the Mahommedans came to India, the Minas seem to have confounded their looking on the boar as an unclean animal with their own regard for it as a sacred animal, and to have been induced in some degree to conform to their faith. Their old idol, however, they still

Parihar Minas.

worshipped, but gave it the Mahommedan name of Father Adam.[10] Subsequently the Saïva Brahmans got hold of them. They did not try to persuade them to give up the worship of Father Adam or of the boar, but simply to allow that Father Adam was a name of Siva, and to worship the cow as well as the boar. Temples were erected in their principal villages, and stones placed in them bearing representations of Siva as Father Adam, of a cow and a boar, and inscriptions to the effect: that the Mahommedans respected the boar and the Hindus the cow, but the true followers of Father Adam respected both; and if they should neglect the worship of any one of the three, the worship of the other two would not benefit them. There are several Saiva temples in the district in which I heard the Brahmans invoke Mahadeva,[11] and the Minas Father Adam.

Moral influence of Brahmans.

Here, too, the Brahmanical influence has been pernicious to the customs of the people. It was an old custom of the Parihars to kill

[10] Adam baba. [11] A name of Siva.

their female infants, the object being, as they said, to avoid the expense of their marriage. But some, who had been more deeply instructed in priestly lore, assured me that when Father Adam's worship was introduced, one of the Minas, who had been most zealous in promoting it, obtained from the god a promise that his sons should be as numerous as the hairs on his body; and, as the divine blessing is generally bestowed through means, he further obtained divine permission for the Parihars to kill their daughters, that so the mothers, being relieved from their nursing, might be sooner able to bear sons. Thus, instead of trying to eradicate a cruel and bad custom, the Brahmans gave it a divine sanction. When English officers some forty years ago visited this district, and tried to put down female infanticide, the strongest objection they met with was the command of Father Adam.

The Bhils.

This propagandism is still active in India. In 1868 an attempt was made to Brahmanize the Bhils of the Aravalis. They agreed to obey the Brahmans, to reverence the cow, to refrain from eating its flesh, and to refuse to eat and drink with their neighbours the Mairs, with whom they had formerly mingled socially. They were thus erected into a Hindu caste, and their idols were received into the Hindu pantheon. In 1869 the famine began; they were without food, and were glad to eat the carcases of their cattle, which were dying. They thus forfeited their new dignity, and apostatized from their new faith. But plenty has now returned, and the attempts to proselytize them are being renewed.

These are specimens of how the Saivas have gone to work; and if the traditions throughout India about Siva and his subordinates were examined, they would probably be found to be skilful adaptations of older objects of worship.[12]

[12] 'In reviewing the state of India during the period which has here been distinguished as the Brahmanical revival, it is impossible to overlook the ecclesiastical organization of the Brahmans, by which the varied populations of India have been brought under their influence and authority. In every village and every important family a Brahman priest is generally established as a preceptor or Purohita. Again, every sect or district is under the jurisdiction of a Guru, or spiritual head,

Forms of Saiva worship.

In nearly all these cases the old form of worship was still maintained. It is almost exclusively among the Saiva sects that the sacrifices of blood, to which I have referred, are offered. But this is accounted for by saying that the god delights in drinking blood and wearing skulls; thus his worship was accommodated to the demon worship of many of the aboriginal tribes. It is more

who maintains its orthodoxy in matters of caste and religion. The Purohita is supported by the village or family where he has taken up his permanent abode. The Guru is generally engaged in extensive ecclesiastical visitations, during which he levies contributions for the support of himself and his own immediate disciples, and confirms the younger Hindus who have attained a suitable age. The missionary operations of the Brahmans are indeed worthy of special study. They have been carried on from time immemorial; and the process is still going on amongst hill tribes and other remote populations. A Brahman makes his appearance in a so-called aboriginal village, and establishes his influence by an affectation of superior sanctity, aided by the fame of his spells, incantations, mystic rites, and astrological predictions. He declares the village idol to be a form of one or other of the great gods or goddesses of the Brahmanical pantheon; and he professes to teach the true forms of worship. He divides the villagers into castes and introduces caste laws. In this manner the populations of India have been brought under the spiritual domination of the Brahmans, and the caste system has been introduced into secluded regions in which it was previously unknown.'—Wheeler's *Hist. of India*, vol. iii. pp. 401, 402.

generally, however, his spouse, under her different names, who is thus honoured. As Mata or Devi she is still worshipped by the sacrifice of goats and buffaloes; as Kali she was formerly worshipped by children being offered to her. As worshippers of her the Thugs were included in the Hindu system; her command and example were cited to make Sati a religious act. It is chiefly through the worship of these goddesses, and such subordinate gods as Bhairon and Khetrpal, that Siva worship maintains its hold of the populace. His own temples are deserted throughout the year, except on the occasion of festivals, and then they are thronged chiefly by wandering devotees.

Secret sects.

One of the worst developments of Sivaism is the rise of secret, or as they call themselves left-handed,[13] sects. These are sects that meet in private, when all rules of caste are for the time set aside, and all eat and drink together; when they meet again in public, caste rules resume their sway. There is reason to believe that in some cases this is only a way of

[13] Bahm Margis.

getting relief from the tyranny of caste; but in many, if not in the majority, of these sects rules of morality share the same fate as the rules of caste.[14] This is especially the case with those called the Sàktas, or the worshippers of Sakti, the female principle. Some of their holy books, called the Tantras, true to the principle of Saiva worship, teach a religion of works, but the works they inculcate are violating the laws of sobriety, decency, and truth. The religion of works and hardship leads to as low an abyss as the religion of devotion and ease.

[14] 'In the Siva cult novices were exposed to every possible allurement and expected to remain unmoved. In the Kali cult nudity was worshipped in Bacchanalian orgies which cannot be described.'—Wheeler.

CHAPTER VI.

RECONCILIATION OF THE SECTS.—REVIEW OF HINDUISM.

Original enmity of the sects.

THE worship of Vishnu and the worship of Siva, then, symbolize originally two opposite, almost antagonistic tendencies of religious thought,—the former regarding Deity as becoming man, with all his imperfections, and requiring to be served as we serve the mighty of our race,—the latter regarding man as by his own exertions freeing himself from all human weaknesses and feelings, and raising himself to the power of the Deity. This antagonism of principles produced a frequent hostility between the rival sects, such as can hardly be explained by the external accidents of their systems. There seems little doubt that Vishnu worship was the older among the Aryan castes at all events. We find in it the continuity of old Brahmanism better preserved, and it has altogether a milder character. This mildness is apparent even in its opposition to Buddhism, and, as shown in the story of the ninth incarnation, it was more ready to amalgamate than to oppose. Sivaism, on the other hand, attacked Buddhism with the vigour of a newer faith and of a nearer relationship. It animated the kings who fought against Buddhism; it was the faith of the fire races of the Rajputs, whose arms finally made Brahmanism triumphant. But the Sivas seem originally to have been opposed to the Vaishnavas as much as to the Buddhists. In the older books of the two sects we find the rival gods denounced, Vishnu banning Siva, and Siva banning Vishnu, each excluding his rival's worshippers from salvation, and consigning them to hell.

Sectarian controversies.

The more popular arguments as to the superiority of the two gods did not indeed turn so much on the deeper questions of their faith as on some traditional incidents. Thus Krishna may have paid his devotions at some shrine of Siva's, or some shrine afterwards identified with his worship. At all events the Saivas preserve the tradition of Krishna's worshipping Siva, and argue that the latter must therefore be the greater god. The Vaishnavas retort, by telling how Siva was unable to protect a certain worshipper of his from Krishna's anger, and how Siva, on the evening after his marriage with Parvati, entertained his bride with an account of Vishnu's incarnation as Rama, and worshipped him as the greatest of gods. These and similar legends are bandied about in this theological warfare.

Reconciliation of the sects.

But by degrees this controversy toned down, though what the causes were we can only surmise. It may have been the necessity of union for triumph over their common enemies the Buddhists; or it may have been the influence of the Vedanta philosophy. At all events we find the principles of this philosophy used to effect a reconciliation: Siva and Vishnu are both one, works are acts of devotion, and acts of devotion are works. Both gods were the same, adapted under different forms to receive different kinds of worship according to different temperaments of men. For popular purposes the union was symbolized by the heads of both gods, with that of Brahma added, being carved out of the same stone. This constitutes the *trimurti*—threefold image—the popular trinity of the Hindus. For the pundits this symbolizes the rivals united in the universal Brahm,—the way of devotion and the way of works united in the way of knowledge. More popularly Brahma is called the creator, Vishnu the preserver, Siva[1] the destroyer; they are also spoken of as past, present, and future. Brahma is thus in both cases made a thing of the past, and his worship has almost entirely disappeared from India. As a matter of fact the worshippers of Vishnu look on him as creator, and destroyer as well as preserver, and so do the worshippers of Siva look on him. The main fact typified was a reconciliation of these two sects.

The trimurti.

There has often been an analogy drawn

Analogy with the Christian trinity.

[1] In this form they receive also the names of Hara, Hari, Har.

between this Hindu and the Christian trinity, but all that can be said of the former is, that it may have been suggested by the latter. There is a chapter in the history of Hinduism that requires yet to be investigated, and that is the influence of early Christianity upon it. We know that in the first ages of the Church the gospel was preached in India, and that it was not without results the existence of the Malabar Christians sufficiently proves. This tells of a movement, of a struggle of some kind, of which all other traces have passed away, but of which the trace may yet be discovered in the effect it produced on Hindu thought. I doubt, however, whether to this Christian teaching we can trace the Hindu conception of the trimurti, not because it is unlikely, but because it comes too late for us to suppose the connection probable. The first indication we find of any attempt to set up the trimurti was in Bijaynagar in the beginning of the fifteenth century,[2]—before the Portuguese had explored the East, and long

[2] Lassen, *Ind. Alt.* vol. iv.

after the influence of earlier Christianity must have ceased to affect India.

The trimurti was possibly an attempt to give greater popular unity to the Hindu faith under the pressure of Mahommedan attack, but the metaphysical basis, on which the union of the sects was attempted, shaped itself under the pressure of the struggle with Buddhism, and received its final form in the early part of the thirteenth century, just when the struggle with Mahommedanism was beginning. It was then that Bopadeva wrote the Bhagavat Purana, which has had more influence on modern Hinduism than any other book. It was written in Sanskrit, but parts of it, especially those relating to the history of Krishna, are translated into most of the modern dialects of India. In it we find the pantheistic doctrine fully developed. Krishna, its hero, is even represented as worshipping Siva, and acknowledging that they were both the same, while Siva acknowledges the power of Krishna as superior to his own. It is in it that the various legends of Vishnu have received their final form, and

Date of the pantheistic reconciliation.

been explained and justified on those pantheistic bases which are now accepted generally throughout India.

Summary. Such is a brief outline of Hinduism and of the various currents of thought and of superstition, which seem to have contributed to its formation. I have not given anything like a full account of it, nor have I even hinted at the existence of many of the gods that enjoy a fair degree of popularity. I have merely described the main features of the system. The reader may fill up the sketch with almost anything he pleases, from monotheism to snail worship, from self-denying beneficence to rapine and murder, and if he only acknowledge the sanctity of the cow and the superiority of the Brahmans, it will be strange if Hinduism cannot find a niche for it. Vishnu and Siva are the two great rivers leading into the ocean of liberation—the Ganges and Indus of religion—and their subordinate deities may be looked on as their tributaries; but there may be as many smaller streams and rills leading to the same end as men choose to imagine.

Review of the work of Hinduism.

We may now review the work that Hinduism has done for India. The Brahmanical revival attacked and conquered Buddhism by laying hold on man's felt need of a superior power, and of all the means of access to it which he had imagined, and adapting them to its own end. We have seen that it took the gods as they were, with all their imperfections and sins, and sought to establish their identity with that universal spirit, or with parts of that universal spirit, which it conceives of as the one existence. Pantheism logically requires that good should be correlated with evil, and Indian pantheism avowedly does so. Human passion naturally leads man to imagine a superior being tainted with the same vices as himself. When the two meet they confirm one another. Pantheism justifies the sinful idol, and the latter nails pantheism down to the practical application of its own principles. Hence in all the Hindu conceptions of the Deity holiness is not an essential; evil may also proceed from Him, and in the popular idols all that is needful is power of a certain kind and to a certain extent. That granted, they may be either angels or devils, patterns of virtue or monsters of vice —the Deity can include both. This is a vice from which Hinduism has never been able to free itself. It has escaped in some instances, as we have seen in the case of Ramanuja and Ramananda, from absolute pantheism. But even Tulsidas, the most popular disciple of the latter and exponent of his system, says, 'I salute everything good, and I salute everything evil.'

Hindu tolerance.

The Hindus often complain of the bigotry and intolerance of Christianity, and contrast with it the charity and tolerance of Hinduism. And truly it would be difficult to get a wider charity, a broader tolerance, than is expressed in the above line. But this very breadth deprives it of all power for good,—makes the good powerless to prevent or repress the evil. This is the fatal defect of Hinduism. It does not exclude good, but it refuses to acknowledge its exclusive claim. There are in Hindu books passages of unsurpassed beauty and purity even, and which one might almost think expressive of the loftiest theistic worship. Yet these passages can influence but little those who read them when they exist alongside of others as vile as these are noble. Nay more, they positively hinder the spread of a pure religion. When the teaching of Christ, for instance, is presented to the Hindus, they acknowledge its purity, and they recognize many of His moral precepts as very like what they have been accustomed to be taught. But they have also been accustomed to hear them along with other teaching as different from them as night from day, or in connection with the worship of beings whose whole lives contradicted them. Of how this may be I have already given one example.[3] Thus, for what hold morality may have on their minds they are indebted to the conscience which God has given them—not in any way to their religion. In it morality is non-essential; and as Buddhism—looked on as a popular system—may be described as 'morality without God,' so Hin-

[3] See *ante*, p. 162.

duism may be described as 'God without morality.'

Blind faith of Hinduism.

Corresponding with this is the principle of the human mind to which Hinduism appeals. We have seen that Hindu philosophy imitates Buddhism in making knowledge the great instrument of salvation. But in the popular religion blind faith takes the place of knowledge, and the only function ascribed to the latter is to discover how the object of worship, whatever that may be, is one with the Supreme. With the majority, however, even this is not necessary. 'Faith is the great thing' is an axiom that comes naturally to the mouth of a Hindu whenever matters of religion are discussed. Faith in the object of your faith, whatever that may be, is considered the sure way of salvation. No matter how morally bad, no matter how utterly contemptible that in which you believe, have faith in it, and you will gain your end. Trust your idol, trust your penances, trust your works, and all will be well. This is a doctrine taught by others besides Hindus, but in the mouth of these latter it has some reason, for it is consistent with their view of the relation of man to God. They do not ignore knowledge altogether, but they give it quite a subsidiary place. From this point of view, as Buddhism may be described as a system of 'knowledge without faith,' so Hinduism may be described as a system of 'faith without knowledge.'

Effects of Hinduism.

Thus has Hinduism spread throughout India, not as a reformation, but as a conservation. It has taken advantage of all existing superstitions, however gross, immoral and criminal, and supplying all with a philosophical basis, has crystallized each into a hardness, and given to the whole a solidarity which makes it now doubly difficult to attack any one of them. It has recognized and vindicated the distinctions of class and tribe, freezing all together instead of fusing all together; making different classes of the same village live together with fewer common sympathies and interests than the French and Germans, making patriotism as we understand it an unknown thing, nationality an impossibility for the Hindus till Hinduism be swept from India. The only thing to be said for it is, that it has conserved some good as well as evil. The law of caste is more binding than the law of conscience, and where the original custom of a caste has been good, it has been preserved. Many who would not refuse to commit an evil because it is forbidden by God, would refuse because it was forbidden by their caste. Thus the restraints of caste have checked the spread of many vices through some classes of society, have enabled them to look on a vice indulged in by others and excuse them for it as being tolerated by their caste, without feeling tempted to indulge in it themselves. This has given a certain stamina to the Hindus which we do not find in other idolaters. But the same thing that thus checks change for evil forbids also change for good. Change is the one point on which Hinduism is intolerant. Let any one ask a Hindu who has been dilating on the intolerance of Christianity and the tolerance of Hinduism, to tolerate one of his caste-fellows practically carrying out his change of belief by change of conduct—acknowledging the one true God by giving up the worship of his caste gods, acknowledging the brotherhood of man by mingling and eating with those of other castes, and he will find that he has roused an intolerance as fierce and unbending as that of the Spanish Inquisition. Hinduism is essentially a quiescent religion, but it was not to be left undisturbed in its hold in India, and we now proceed to its struggles with other faiths.

PART III.

HINDUISM AND MAHOMMEDANISM.

HINDUISM AND MAHOMMEDANISM.

THE first hostile faith with which Hinduism had to contend after its triumph over Buddhism was Mahommedanism, and the story of this contest is one of the most remarkable and instructive chapters in the history of religion. The struggle was long and arduous, but the main features may be easily apprehended, and as the chief object of our study is rather the relations of Hinduism to Christianity, I will be brief.

Mahommedanism took its rise with the preaching of Mahommed in Arabia in the beginning of the sixth century. It was a strong monotheism, and its brief creed was, 'There is no God but God, and Mahommed is the prophet of God.' Its founder was acquainted with the Jewish and Christian Scriptures, and acknowledged them as in- Rise of Mahommedanism. Its principles.

spired, but he maintained the superior authority of the Koran, which he was commissioned to impart to the world. He allowed that Moses and the prophets and Jesus were all prophets sent by God, but he was the last and greatest, and superseded them all. He had in his travels while a young man had occasion to observe the various sects of Christians and the offensive prominence and almost material interpretation that was given to the doctrine of the Trinity, and he denounced that doctrine as an abomination. He likewise denounced not only all image worship, but the making of images for any purpose, as a sin, though he was obliged to give way to the old Arab superstition of worshipping the Kabah at

Way of salvation.

Mecca.[1] Salvation he taught was to be obtained by works, by holding the true faith, by repeating the above creed, by praying

[1] This is simply a black stone—possibly an aërolite—that is in the Mosque at Mecca. A learned Maulvi seriously maintained to me that its worship was not a breach of the second Commandment, on the ground that it was not the likeness of anything in the heaven above, on the earth beneath, or in the water under the earth. The same might be said of nearly all the Hindu idols.

five times daily, by performing daily ablutions, by fasting in the month Ramzan from sunrise to sunset daily, by giving a fortieth of one's goods in charity, by making the pilgrimage to Mecca, and, above all, by dying in war for the propagation of the faith. The morality he inculcated was loose, but it **Morality.** was an improvement on that of the Arabs among whom he lived. He forbade the use of wine, but he sanctioned polygamy and concubinage. The sinfulness of sin is indeed no part of his system; repentance, as explained by him, does not imply hatred or renouncement of sin, and this defect becomes more glaring in the teaching of his followers. In Mahommedan theology knowledge takes precedence of holiness, and what we call the fall of man rather raised him in the scale of being, by giving him knowledge.[2] God is thus ultimately made the author of sin in man, and this vice taints and weakens the whole system. Its great merit and its great power is its strong assertion of the Unity of God.

[2] See Appendix D.

Spread of Mahommedanism.

At first its progress was slow, and it was not till Mahommed adopted the sword as a means of conversion, till the charms of military enthusiasm and political ascendancy were added to those of poetry and eloquence, that his religion became a power. Then it spread with lightning speed. The Arabs, brought by their religion for the first time into the community of nations, and stirred up by their religious enthusiasm to be invincible soldiers, were everywhere victorious. After victory their propaganda was simple enough—to the 'people of the book,' the Christians and Jews, they gave the choice—become Mahommedans or pay tribute; to idolaters—become Mahommedans or die. A political ascendancy thus accompanied Mahommedanism wherever it spread, which proved an irresistible argument for all those whose faith was otherwise weak; and when they had once joined the profession of 'the faithful,' the charms of war and conquest transformed them into zealous propagandists of the new faith. Mahommedanism is a religion of the sword, and has spread almost exclusively by its means.

Spread of Mahommedanism in India.

Shortly after the death of Mahommed the Arabs made some incursions into India, but it was not till the beginning of the eighth century that they made any serious attempt on it. In the year 705 A.D. Walid conquered Sind, and in subsequent years his armies advanced as far as the Ganges. His general Kasim conquered Gujerat, and attacked Chitor, the capital of Mewar. But here the progress of the victorious Moslem was stayed. They were defeated and driven out of India by Bappa, the founder of the race of kings who to this day sit on the Mewar throne. It was not for a hundred years thereafter that they again attempted its subjugation, and then again they were encountered by the Raja of the same kingdom, at the head of the chivalry of India, who flocked to his banner, and, after being defeated twenty-four times, were once more fairly driven out of the land. For a hundred and fifty years again the Mahommedans desisted from serious attempts, but, in the beginning of the eleventh century, the celebrated Mahmùd of Ghazni invaded India twelve times, and was everywhere victorious, compelling the native princes to submit or driving them from their thrones. He left traces of his victorious progress in the idols he broke and the temples he plundered. But his career was like that of the hurricane, passing through the land but not remaining in it. Within fifteen years after his death the Hindus had risen under Visala Deva, king of Ajmer, and driven his successors beyond the Sutledge; and for a hundred and fifty years longer India remained the *Arya vartta,* the land of the pure Aryas. It was not till the end of the twelfth century that the victories of Mahommed Ghori established Mahommedan supremacy in India.

Cause of the resistance of India to Mahommedanism.

Thus while the Mahommedan power had spread with unmatched rapidity over Syria and Persia, along the north of Africa, and into Spain, it for six hundred years failed to overcome the compact resistance offered by India. But the cause of this is not far to seek. In the lands where it first spread, Christianity had sapped the old faiths, and had in its turn been so much contaminated by them that its pristine vigour had decayed. It inspired its followers neither with the tenacity of an ancient faith nor with the enthusiasm of a new one, so that they succumbed easily to the fresh vigour of Islam. In India, on the other hand, Hinduism had just triumphed under the great Brahmanical revival. After having, as we have seen, been nearly quenched by Buddhism, it had in its turn risen up and extirpated it from the Peninsula. The Hindus were thus attached to their faith with all the strength which pride in its antiquity and enthusiasm on account of its fresh triumphs could inspire, and when a head arose to combine the various states, to give unity to their strength and direction to their valour, they proved too strong even for the fanaticism of Islam.

Mahommedan conquest of India.

But jealousies and rivalries among the Hindu princes, fanned by caste feelings and teaching, produced destructive internecine wars, which left them a prey at last to the Mahommedan invaders. At the end of the twelfth century they had conquered all North India, and their military supremacy was established. The Mahommedans had triumphed, but Mahommedanism did not. Their first zeal had so far abated, that they admitted idolaters too to the payment of tribute, and this the Hindus were content to pay where they could not throw off the yoke of the oppressor. Many Hindu kings maintained their independence, and made war against the invaders with varying success, till at last the genius of Akbar established the Mahommedan dominion on a secure basis.

Akbar's policy.

This basis, however, consisted in depriving Mahommedanism of its political privileges. He abolished the tax on infidels, which Hindus who would not profess Mahommedanism had to pay; and thus made all his subjects equal in the eye of the law, no difference being allowed on account of their religious creed. He also united himself by marriage with some of the noblest royal houses of India, and thus attached them to his throne. He had no very firm religious creed himself, and set himself with the indifference of a philosopher and the zeal of a politician to assimilate the religious beliefs of his subjects. While indifferent to the special claims of Mahommed, he fostered the lower forms of his religion, and especially the worship of saints,—a corruption that had long been gaining ground in Islam. The tombs of saints all over the country were sought out, mosques erected over them, and legends with regard to them invented or garnished up. This policy was so far successful that the Hindus did begin to worship many of their saints, and unite with the Mahommedans in paying them reverence on their great festivals. The political result too was obtained in so far as the stability of his own throne was concerned, both creeds uniting to support it, but the effect on Mahommedanism itself was disastrous. Mahommedanism, as a quiescent non-proselytizing religion, could only become corrupt and rotten. The effect of all this policy on the mass of Mahommedans was to deprive their religious sentiment of that intolerance which constituted its strength. Its moral power was gone when it ceased to be intolerant.

Policy of Aurangzèb.

Yet this policy preserved the Mogul empire in its integrity for upwards of a hundred years, till the principle and policy of intolerance revived in Aurangzèb. He reimposed the poll-tax on infidels, and thereby again branded all his Hindu subjects with inferiority on account of their religious beliefs. This alienated them, and ultimately drove them into rebellion. He decreed the destruction of idols; and the prince of Mewar offered 'the heads of one hundred thousand Rajputs' for the defence of one of the most popular of these idols, thus making it the symbol of Hindu nationality. The rebellion often seemed crushed, but it maintained itself with the vitality which only a struggle for religion could inspire, and imparted in turn a vitality to that religion which only exertion, sacrifice and suffering could beget. The Hindus were driven to emulate the intolerance of their opponents, —shaving the Kazis, destroying the mosques, throwing the Korans into wells, and forbidding the call to prayer wherever they had power. This gave room for the Mahratta power to rise in the south,—a Hindu power, though based on plunder; and when Aurangzèb, the ablest of the Moguls, died, he saw the empire breaking up on every side. In about thirty years it received its death-blow from another Mahommedan power, the Persians under Nadir Shah. Thereafter the Hindu states either assumed their old independence or established new dominions; while the Mahommedan emperor, still their nominal head, became more and more a mere puppet in their hands. Now the last traces of that empire have passed away: the last representative of Mahommedan supremacy ended his days a convict in a penal settlement. Of the native princes now in alliance with the British Government, only one or two of any importance are Mahommedans: of the 220 millions who inhabit India, about fifty millions belong to that religion. Of these, about twenty millions in Bengal are the descendants of the lowest class of Hindus, who adopted this faith to gain a higher social standing, and the rest are descendants of the old Patthan and Mogul conquerors. But they are nearly all now in a low social position as compared with the Hindus; they are more backward in taking advantage of the educational[3] and

3 Of twenty-one millions of Mahommedans in Bengal, only twenty-eight thousand attend Government schools.

other benefits which the British offer, and are sinking lower morally and socially. That is the external history of Mahommedanism in India.

Effect of Mahommedanism on Hinduism.

Turning to the internal history, the first inquiry is as to the effect which it has had on Hinduism itself, what modification it has produced on the faith of the Hindus; and the answer is, almost none. It seems a strange conclusion to come to that a powerful religion like Mahommedanism should have been for six centuries in India, and produced no effect on the belief of the majority of its population. Yet such is undoubtedly the fact. The chief instrument of Mahommedan conversion is the sword: this may produce an outer acquiescence, it may even ultimately force multitudes to adopt alike the profession and faith of Mahommedanism, but it cannot produce any modification in a hostile faith, least of all could it do so in India. While war and conquest and violence were raging about it, Hinduism was steadily developing itself.

> 'The East bow'd low before the blast,
> In patient deep disdain;

She let the legions thunder past,
And plunged in thought again.'

The only difference we can now trace is that the theory and system of Bopa Deva,[4] which before the Mahommedan conquest was accepted only by the Brahmans, has now pervaded nearly every caste of Hindus. Take any of the points of difference between Mahommedanism and Hinduism, and it will be found that in these Hinduism is stronger and more intolerant than it was before its rival appeared in India. Image worship is as general and as devoutly believed in, and caste as tyrannical as before the Mussulman conquerors set their foot in India, while the pantheistic principles on which they are justified are much more extensively diffused. The doctrine of a Supreme God above and beyond Vishnu, Siva, and the other deities, which some have looked upon as the effect of Mahommedan influence, is a result rather of Hindu philosophy. It was developed before the Mahommedans entered India, and even the theistic

[4] See *ante*, p. 211.

protest against pantheism was anterior to their conquest.[5]

Deteriorating effects.

In some of the sects which were developed from the last named movement we no doubt do see the influence of the foreign faith,—most notably in the Kavir Pantis; but the adherents of these sects are comparatively few in number, and they have themselves relapsed generally into pantheistic idolatry, from which they could never entirely disentangle themselves. The general effect of Mahommedanism on Hinduism has been rather of a deteriorating character. The greater licentiousness of its followers has led to the greater degradation of women among the Hindus. They have not now the same freedom and respect given to them, which the older books of India show they once had, and this change the Hindus attribute to the license of their Mahommedan conquerors.

[5] Ramanuja lived certainly not later than the beginning of the twelfth century, while the Mahommedan conquest took place at the end of it. If we place Bopa Deva in the thirteenth century, as Lassen does, we have the remarkable fact of pantheistic idolatry developing and strengthening itself in the face of victorious monotheists.

An indirect effect of this has been the increase of these secret sects, which are the greatest stain on modern Hinduism.

Effect of Hinduism on Mahommedanism.

The bad influence which Hinduism has experienced from Mahommedanism is nothing, however, compared with the deteriorating influence of Hinduism on Mahommedanism. It has now degenerated in most of its adherents in India to be little more than a caste of Hinduism. They have their caste rules, as strong and as binding as their Hindu brethren. Their priests repeat the verses of the Koran as the Brahmans repeat the hymns of the Vedas, with just as little idea of their meaning. Their worship of Allah—the one God—is a mere form; their real worship is paid to the saints: offerings are brought to their tombs, or gifts given to the priests who officiate in the mosques erected in their honour. Their religion is indeed known in India as saint-worship,[6] while that of the Hindus is image-worship,[7] and this for the majority of both creeds is the practical difference. Even in this however they are

[6] Pir parasti. [7] But parasti.

not exclusive; the Hindus join cordially in the festivals in honour of some of the greater Mahommedan saints, and in some places the Mahommedans join in those in honour of Hindu idols. The latter do differ from the former in that they occasionally still attempt to proselytize, but for the old power of the sword they now use the enticements of marriage. If a Hindu should become enamoured of a Mussulman girl, that is made the means of decoying him away from his former caste and joining her co-religionists, and he gains his wife at the expense of becoming a Mahommedan,—a change of name and of companions without any change of life, faith, or worship.

Present position. Triumph of Hinduism.

These two religions have thus settled down beside one another on terms of mutual charity and *toleration.* This does not imply any great change or deterioration in Hinduism, for its principles admit every belief as truth, every religion as a way of salvation. All that it requires is acknowledgment of the same principle from other religions, and abstinence from efforts at winning or forcing from it its own adherents. This is the position which Hinduism has practically forced Mahommedanism to assume in India. But such a position is ruinous for the latter religion. When it has lost the power and principle of expansion it must wither and die. What does it avail it that its votaries repeat the formula 'There is no God but God,' when they have no means to force that truth on others? The Hindus too acknowledge that there is one Supreme Lord, and their idol-worship they believe bears the same relation to their worship of Him as the saint-worship of the Mussulmans does to their worship of Allah. Mahommedanism is thus now utterly weak and powerless beside Hinduism, and the longer it accepts this position the weaker must its power become over its own disciples.

Mahommedan revival.

A Mahommedan revival has indeed been going on for some time, but not sufficiently long to enable us to predict its ultimate results. It is mostly a political movement. It does not protest against saint-worship nor against caste exclusiveness. It is rather a protest against European enlightenment and civilization. It is directed more against the supremacy of the hated infidel than against the idolatry of the Hindus or the corruptions of the followers of the Prophet themselves. Its object is to inspire the great mass of the Mussulmans with that bigotry and exclusiveness which Persian and Arabic literature has cherished in the educated few, and to prepare the way for another holy war. But the opportunity of Mahommedanism becoming the religion of India has passed. Hinduism has vanquished it by the sheer force of inertia.

PART IV.

HINDUISM AND CHRISTIANITY.

HINDUISM AND CHRISTIANITY.

HINDUISM has thus triumphed over two of the great missionary religions of the world,[1] that of Buddha and that of Mahommed; the contest has now begun with the third,—that of Christ. The Church of Christ is seeking by its missions to convert India to Him. Is this a work to be undertaken with hope or with doubt, one which it would be wise to persevere in or to abandon? The command of our Lord—His marching orders, as the Duke of Wellington said to a somewhat sceptical chaplain,—'Go ye into all the world, and preach the Gospel to every creature,' is a sufficient warrant for the Church to continue her work, a sufficient guarantee that the truth which He embodied and which he bade His disciples preach is the best suited for the Hindu as for all nations.

Contest between Christianity and Hinduism begun.

[1] See Max Müller's *Lecture on Missions*.

Conditions of the contest.

But it is well also carefully to examine the conditions of the contest, to see what are the strong and what the weak points in the enemy's line of defence ; by what tactics and with what arms we may best conquer it, and what reasons we have, from the past history and present state of Hinduism, to hope for success. In conducting this examination we will first compare the principles of the Christian and of the Hindu faiths, their points of approach and their points of antagonism; then look at the attempts that are being made to reform Hinduism independently of Christianity; and lastly, consider the attitude which the Church must preserve to secure final triumph.

CHAPTER I.

AFFINITIES AND ANTAGONISMS OF CHRISTIANITY AND HINDUISM.

Elements of natural religion in both systems.

HERE we must beware of taking natural religion for either Hinduism or Christianity. The sentiment of dependence on a higher power and the teaching of conscience exist more or less strongly in all men, leading them to learn the lessons of nature and prompting a worship recognized as true by true religion. 'He left not Himself without a witness, in that He did good, and gave us rain from heaven, and fruitful seasons, filling our hearts with food and gladness.'[1] 'The Gentiles, having not the law, are a law unto themselves: who show the works of the law written in their hearts.'[2] In the literature of every nation that has produced a literature we find these sentiments expressed, man giv-

[1] Acts xiv. 17. [2] Rom. ii. 14, 15.

ing utterance to those feelings of reverence, trust and truth, which show that the image of God within him, though defaced, is not destroyed. In the literature of no heathen nation probably is this found more abundantly than in that of the Hindus. It contains multitudes not only of stray verses, but even whole hymns, in which a Christian might express many of his feelings of devotion.[3] All these Christianity gladly welcomes as proofs of its congruity with natural religion, but they are not Christianity. Hinduism also uses them, but they are not Hinduism.

True grounds of comparison, their teaching about sin.

Properly to compare the two religions we must look not only at their teaching with regard to God and man, but also at their teaching with regard to God and the sinner. That he is a sinner, that he has sinned, that he does sin, man's conscience bears witness. How may man, having sinned, be just with God? How will God deal with sinful man? These are questions which man as a religious being is forced to face; these are the

[3] See Appendix E, Natural Religion in Indian Literature.

questions which the various religions of the world seek to answer, and their answers to which modify and distinguish their views both of God and of man. These also are the questions on which Hinduism joins issue with Christianity. Yet even in them we may find many points of resemblance, just sufficient indeed to make the antagonism sharper and more direct. In Hinduism the same wants and instincts are expressed as those which Christianity professes to satisfy. But Hinduism also professes to satisfy them with what is often liker a hideous caricature of the Christian solution, than any counterpart to it.

Distinction between Hindu and Christian principles.

To show more clearly the relative positions of Hinduism and Christianity, I must recur to the distinctions which I have already drawn between their higher principles.[4] Christianity teaches the personality, Hinduism the impersonality of God. Christianity makes holiness an essential in God and His government, Hinduism makes it an accident. These distinctions, carried along the whole

[4] See *ante*, p. 113.

line of teaching of the two faiths, make their points of approach points of antagonism; and as these are true or false must either system win or lose.

Salvation. Both religions teach that salvation is the chief end of man, and that to show the way of salvation is the chief end of religion. The same word which the Hindus use to express their idea of man's final end is the word used by the translators of the Bible to express the Christian salvation. Salvation may also be said in both systems to include the idea of liberation, but in Hinduism the liberation sought is deliverance from personal existence, in Christianity deliverance from sin.

Hindu and Christian conceptions. The Hindu idea of salvation is that of a man crossing a broad stream. He occasionally steps on rocks, fords shallows, swims through currents. He may sometimes be swept back from the shore towards which he is struggling, sometimes borne nearer to it; but the stream is something entirely distinct from him: he looks merely to getting through it and out of it. He does not look to any change in himself. The Christian idea is rather that of a man who is smitten with a deadly disease from which he seeks to be quit. The disease affects his whole frame, prevents him acting vigorously, menaces him with death. His object is to get the disease out of him—to be restored to a healthy natural state. Christianity teaches that man is sinful; for it teaches that there is a personal God, whose holy law man has failed to obey. Deliverance from this failure, from this sin, and a consequent eternal life of holy service, it teaches to be salvation. Hinduism, as we have seen, is debarred from this conception, for it denies a personal God; denying Him, it can have no place for His holy law, and consequently sin as such is excluded also. Hinduism accordingly teaches that salvation is not deliverance from sin any more than deliverance from holiness. Sin, as we conceive it, is not sin any more than the current that sweeps the swimmer into danger is sin. It in fact ought to have no place in the Hindu religion at all. But it has a place. Neither the word nor the idea of sin is strange to the Hindu. It does not need any long argument to show him that it must be punished. Why is this? Simply because the higher principles of Hinduism will not square with human conscience and consciousness. They are at enmity with the natural law written on the hearts of all men, as much as with Christianity. Hinduism has tried to escape from this antagonism by allowing sin as an inferior calamity, and deliverance from it as an inferior stage of salvation, but the fact that it admits sin at all is fatal to its conception of the higher salvation.

Way of salvation.

But it is when we come to the way of salvation that the resemblances and contrasts of the two religions become most striking. In both we find the idea of vicarious atonement, of the incarnation, and of striving to be like God. In the Christian faith they are all united in Christ, whose person gives to them a harmony, and a fulness of grace and truth, which man has, since His appearance, been ever studying, but never able fully to measure. In Hinduism these truths, severed one from the other, as from their true centre, have become corrupted and powerless, as limbs severed from the living body.

It has often been said that the most distinctive doctrine of Christianity is that of vicarious atonement for sin; but this is also a doctrine of Hinduism. The truth taught in the Bible is, that Christ is the vicarious atonement for sin. He says of Himself, 'The Son of Man came not to be ministered unto, but to minister, and to give His life a ransom for many.'[5] This is the great doctrine which the apostles constantly pressed. 'When we were yet without strength, in due time Christ died for the ungodly.'[6] 'Christ also hath once suffered for sins, the just for the unjust, that He might bring us to God.'[7] There is here a recognition that sin separates from God, that it must be removed, and its penalty borne, ere the at-one-ment can be made, that it is borne by one himself sinless. There is a voluntary offering on the part of the substitute, and there must be a voluntary acceptance on the part of the sinner. In this the sinfulness of sin and the love of the person who bears the

Vicarious atonement; Christian doctrine.

[5] Matt. xx. 28. [6] Rom. v. 6. [7] 1 Pet. iii. 8.

sin are both exhibited, and become motives for man to strive after holiness.

Objections to the Christian doctrine.

But the idea of one man thus suffering for the crime of another is an injustice. It is a monstrosity which no court of justice, except in very inferior stages of enlightenment, would tolerate, even with the freest and most voluntary offering and acceptance of the substitution. It is further an encouragement to sin, by letting the sinner fancy that he will be freed from its consequences, or, if it does not destroy the sense of justice in man, it will cause him a greater torture than it delivers him from, by making him feel that his sins have caused suffering to one who did not deserve it. There is therefore in this substitution neither justice nor mercy. Such are the objections that have been principally urged against the Christian idea of atonement; but before noticing how Christianity meets them, it will be well to look at how Hinduism has met them, for its fate may well serve as a warning to those who attempt to solve such problems on the analogy of human law.

Hindu doctrine.

Hinduism still retains the conception of

vicarious atonement. Originally, we have seen, the true idea of substitution was typified in sacrifice; but the unsatisfying nature of this, and possibly also the desire to meet such objections as the above, present in the mind though not formally expressed, led the Hindus to look for atonement each in himself. Hence this sentiment found satisfaction in the transmigration of souls, which, ever since Buddha's time, has, in Hindu thought, taken the place of sacrifice as the atonement for sin. But this is practically vicarious atonement, for the element of consciousness separates the person who sins from the person who suffers. He is said to be the same, but he does not know who or what he was before, or what the sins were whose penalty he is now suffering. There is thus a real substitution, but it is quite involuntary on both sides. The Hindu is both the atoner and the atoned for. What he suffers now he suffers on account of sins committed by himself in a previous birth, that is, by another; and these sufferings he has no choice but to endure. Nay, further, the Hindus are thoroughly con-

Transmigration virtually vicarious.

sistent in recognizing that continuing in sin is the punishment of sin, for they say that the very sins a man now commits are punishments of previous, that is, of another's sins; and he cannot but commit them. Their punishment again he cannot bear in his present birth if he would, they must be borne by him in another birth, when the loss of all consciousness of the present has made him in fact another person. But not only does he thus involuntarily atone for another's sin, he also involuntarily atones for another's virtue. His present happiness is the reward of a previous person's good deeds, his present good deeds will be rewarded to some future person. In all this there is an absence of that amount of justice which the free action of the will secures in the Christian system; sin is not made exceeding sinful, but merely a misfortune, differing accidentally from virtue; the sense of responsibility is destroyed; the power of the will annihilated, the discipline of suffering lost; the work is never completed or approaching completion, but goes on through an unending series of atonements. Thus the

Moral failure of this doctrine.

Hindu doctrine, trying to escape vicarious atonement, has only imposed one of iron necessity, instead of one of free offer and free acceptance; one which, instead of being a stimulus to man to struggle against sin and for holiness, is rather a dead weight, tending to make him look on all such struggle as hopeless.

How does Christianity meet the difficulty? By affirming the truth, of which we have seen that Brahmanism in its earlier stages retained a perception, that the substitute is God Himself. It vindicates the justice and moral power of vicarious atonement by the fact of the Incarnation. It teaches that 'the Word was God,'[8] 'was made flesh and dwelt among us;'[9] that in His humanity He once for all put away sin by the sacrifice of Himself;[10] that 'whosoever believeth on Him should not perish, but have everlasting life.'[11] The truth here affirmed transcends our comprehension, as do the ultimate causes of nearly all the facts of nature, which we nevertheless accept as truths; and it is supplemented by other doctrines, such as the union between

The Christian solution, the Incarnation.

[8] John i. 1. [9] John i. 14. [10] Heb. ix. 26. [11] John iii. 16.

Christ and believers, which it would be foreign to my purpose here to enter on. I would dwell merely on the ethical aspect of the question, and seek to show that the Incarnation solves the difficulties of vicarious atonement, in attempting to solve which Hinduism has so signally failed, and restores harmony and consistency to what is otherwise discordant and irreconcileable.

Sin, non-trust of God.

What is sin, for which atonement has to be made? It is breaking God's moral law. This law, as regards the relation of the creature to the Creator, of man to his Maker, is ultimately trust; and the breaking of it is ultimately non-trust. Whether it be called disobedience or setting up man's own will in opposition to the Divine will, it finally resolves itself into this. Offences against fellow-men follow, but the root of the whole, for which a remedy has to be provided, is this rupture in the law of our relation to God. The most obvious remedy for this would be, for man to trust God as he did before. But the fact that he has distrusted God stands in the way.

Distinction between Divine and human law.

If the laws of God had been as the laws of man, arbitrary enactments of certain punishments for certain offences, that could be enforced or set aside at pleasure, it might have been possible for man to revert to his original position, and the fact of his distrust might have been a mere episode to be soon forgotten: no atonement would have been needed. But the laws of God, in so far as known to us, are necessary sequences, as that the fruit springs from the seed, that a man must reap what he has sown. Man could not sin without reaping the fruit of sin. And what is this fruit? Just being and continuing sinful. Sin is severing the bond of trust that binds man to God; its punishment is remaining with that bond severed. Suffering and sorrow are secondary consequences of this, but the great penalty of sin is to continue sinning, to continue sowing the seeds of sorrow, and to lose the power of holiness, the power of sowing the seeds of happiness. This truth the Hindus recognise when they say that their present sins are the fruits of former evil deeds. Any remedy to be effectual must remove the root of the evil.

Christian remedy for sin, trust in God.

And what is the remedy which Christianity offers? It simply teaches man, in the very consequences of his non-trust, to trust God. Man after sinning could not trust God merely for what he had trusted Him before. By doing so he would leave all the elements introduced by his sin outside the range of his trust, and these would still remain elements of discord between him and his Maker, producing an ever-widening breach, the course, as we have seen, which Hinduism has taken. Trusting to a simple forgiveness would be trusting to a suspension instead of a fulfilment of God's law, would be distrust under the pretence of trust. The Gospel, however, reveals the fact that God has met the conditions imposed by man's sin; that, becoming man, He has borne its penalty. When man trusts God to bear this penalty, as he trusts Him for life and everything else, he brings the antidote to the very root of the disease. Trust being restored in the very part of man's relations most antagonistic to trust—in the consequences of non-trust—it follows naturally in everything else. Obedience follows faith.

This is why the Gospel is 'Believe in Christ' —God incarnate—rather than 'Believe in God.' The latter is the duty of man as man; the former is the duty of man as a sinner. Trust is the fit relation of the creature to the Creator; the Gospel says, carry that same trust into the very position in which you have been placed by sin.

This leaves difficulties to be explained on the Divine side of the question as great as ever, and seems even to imply that God, in bearing man's sin, was separated from Himself. This is just what Christianity accepts, and what Mrs. Browning has expressed as boldly and truly as beautifully in the words:

This removes not the metaphysical,

'Deserted! God would separate from His own essence rather,
And Adam's sins have swept between the righteous Son and Father.
Yea, once Emmanuel's orphan cry this universe hath shaken;
It went up single, echoless, "My God, I am forsaken."'

I do not enter on the discussion of these difficulties, which have nothing to do with the question in hand,—the ethical question as to how the Incarnation removes the moral but the ethical difficulty.

difficulties of vicarious atonement. It is no more shocking to the sense of justice or to devout feeling in man, to trust God to bear the penalty of his sin, than it is to trust Him for life or anything for which he is dependent on Him. It requires a much greater exertion of faith and will to do this, but the very fact that it does so makes trust follow necessarily in everything else. Christ's atonement, then, destroys sin by enabling man to trust God for the very reparation of his non-trust, and harmony being restored on this point, the Divine law of sequence necessitates its being restored in man's whole nature. When the two are taken together, as they are in the Christian system, vicarious atonement is seen to be righteous and effective, and an adequate reason is supplied for the Incarnation.

Hindu doctrine of the Incarnation.

In Hinduism, on the other hand, as we have seen that the doctrine of vicarious atonement, separated from that of the Incarnation, is contradictory and powerless; so too, in that system, the doctrine of the Incarnation, disconnected with that of vicarious atonement, is meaningless and contemptible.

No such connection could exist when man had to atone for his own sin in a reproduction of his own self. The Hindu conception of the Incarnation is, therefore, only an evidence of the aspiration of the human soul after God and of its inability to supply that want by any fiction of its own. It could not realize a work done once and done perfectly. The same deity, as we have seen, is said to have become incarnate many times, and in animals as well as in man. On each occasion it is to put right something that has gone wrong in the ordinary history of the world, to destroy a dangerous tribe, to kill a tyrannical king, to do deeds that might have been as well done by men, and less wonderful than many that have been done by men. There is no conception of any of them bearing for man what man could not bear himself. His very incarnations are spoken of as the consequences of deeds he had himself performed; one was the fruit of sins he had committed, another of a curse that had been pronounced on him. Yet even to such a being human instinct has led his worshippers to turn for deliverance. Hopeless themselves of being able to reach the end of their long chain of births, they look to him to deliver them from it, but not by delivering them from sin, only by so absorbing them in himself, that they may perform sin and holiness, and reap joy or sorrow in him, till all such things shall have ceased. Even for the attainment of this boon they have no security. It is not even pretended that any one of their avatars, by triumphing over death, has given evidence of his abiding power to save his worshippers.

Striving to be like God.

The last point of resemblance and contrast between the two religions which I have indicated is—striving after likeness to God. This in the Christian religion cannot be dissociated from the doctrine of the Incarnation. The Christian system is like an arch, in which all the parts are mutually dependent, resting on man a sinner on one side, and on man made like to God on the other. The Incarnation of Christ is the keystone which gives compactness to the whole, and the removal of which would cause

Christian conception.

the whole to collapse. As one side of the Incarnation looks towards the atonement of man's sin, the other looks to perfecting him in the likeness of God. As it effects the former by restoring trust in God, it effects the latter by revealing the character of God. Jesus Christ was a revelation of perfect holiness and spotless purity. Power, as man understands it, was indeed present in His miracles, but the power which He most divinely manifested was the power of holiness, goodness and truth. He is thus an example of that holiness, that union with God and likeness to Him, the attainment of which should be the end of all religion. It has been attained once in the history of man, and thus the obligation of it on all men has been shown. 'Ye shall be holy, for I am holy,' was a call not to mere ceremonial purification, but to that holiness of life which Christ perfectly exemplified. And this holiness the Gospel teaches is to be attained by an extension of that principle of trust which we have seen vicarious atonement restores to man. The Divine Spirit is promised to aid those who seek to be holy as Christ was, and those who trust Christ for forgiveness are led, as a consequence, to trust His Spirit for power to be like Him. This likeness the Bible teaches to consist in a perfectly holy life, in striving after perfect conformity with God's will even in the most ordinary actions of daily life. 'Whether therefore ye eat or drink, or whatsoever ye do, do all to the glory of God.' Thus the holiness of heaven will be a completion of the obedience begun on earth.

Hindu counterpart.

We find a counterpart to all this in Hinduism, but it is the arch without the keystone, and consequently in fragments and ruins. God-like life could scarcely start from the examples of the incarnations, for none of their lives is superhuman in so far as holiness is concerned. Even Rama, the most blameless character conceived in Hindu literature, religious or profane, is by no means perfect; while the most popularly worshipped incarnation, we have seen, committed deeds so vile, that even the narrator warns his hearers *not* to take him for their example.[12] It is accordingly well worthy of remark, that the idea of striving to attain to likeness with the Deity has no place among those sects of Hindus, who trust to or believe in incarnations of the Deity. The Saivas, who deny the incarnations, are the sectaries who seek to work out a likeness to God and a union with Him by their own lives. This is their whole religion, and there are no incarnations to whom they look for atonement or for substitution. But, without the Divine example of One who has come down from above, they seek to attain divinity by destroying instead of perfecting humanity, by mortifying all human desires and inclinations, as well as all sinful desires and inclinations. They cannot conceive anything god-like in the faithful discharge of 'the daily round, the common task;' their conception of being god-like is to be quit of these altogether. The result of this process is rather to destroy what remaining goodness there is

[12] See *ante*, p. 161. The sage follows up the pantheistic vindication there given with the advice: 'Listen to the story of Hari, but do not think of doing his deeds.'

in man. It is needful to have seen some of those whom the Hindus look on as their most holy men, approaching in their perfection most nearly to God, to understand how loathsome this conception may become.

Difficulties occasioned by these resemblances.

We thus see, that to the main doctrines of Christianity Hinduism presents counterparts, which show how unable the human heart is to do without something to fill the void occasioned by its own aspirations, and which, therefore, encourage us to offer the true satisfaction for them, in the hope that it will be recognised and accepted. But they show also the extreme arduousness of the task. It is not a void that we have to fill, not an empty position that we have to occupy, but one already held by a powerful foe. The very amount of similarity in the opposite doctrines tends to give greater bitterness to the moral antagonism that divides them, and to make Hindus, after hearing an exposition of Christian truth, turn back to their own tenets, with the conviction that they are fundamentally the same, and much better suited for them.

And this feeling is intensified by another.

Had it only been with the theology of Hinduism that Christianity had to fight, its converts might by this time have numbered millions. It is in its anthropology, its doctrine about man, that the great strength of the Hindu system lies. On this question Hinduism has not a single point of contact with Christianity. It is in utter, entire opposition. Christianity teaches the universal brotherhood of man; Hinduism teaches the divine order, the binding obligation of caste. This we have seen is the last result of its doctrine of impersonality and transmigration,—to deny the unity of the human race. At this we need not be surprised. Hinduism developed itself in opposition to Buddhism, which, as well as the Christian religion, was a religion of humanity, and it is natural that Hinduism should be strongest on those points in which it had to struggle most decisively against it.

Antagonism of Christian and Hindu anthropology.

Caste is therefore in reality the greatest strength of Hinduism; the most active foe with which Christianity has to contend. Practical social interests here come in to give vitality to

Caste produces

Antipathy, religious dogma. The equality and brotherhood of mankind is as hateful a doctrine to the Hindus as was the idea of the equality of the Negro and European race to the planters of America; and as in India it is the distinctive social doctrine of a hostile creed, it makes them look with suspicion and dislike on all its other teaching. Even when they have been induced to study the Christian religion, and have become convinced of its truth and excellence, of the divinity and moral holiness of its Founder, they have not been able to accept the idea of all men being brethren, of the sweeper being naturally the same as the Brahman, and able through education and training to rise to the same social position.

Terrorism, If they do overcome their repugnance to this thought, and become convinced of its truth, the terrible social persecution and ostracism, which they would have to endure in practically carrying it out, most frequently prove too strong for their convictions, and hold them bound to follow customs which they condemn, to worship gods in whom they disbelieve. If they take the final step of renouncing caste, then caste takes its final step of renouncing them. They are cut off Isolation. from Hindu society, they are forbidden to live with their families or mingle with their relatives. The funeral rites are sometimes performed for them, and their wives assume widows' weeds. Christians are for the Hindus only an additional caste; Christianity is their system of belief and practice, all the more abominable that it interferes with other castes. Native Christians are thus nearly as much isolated from the mass of their countrymen as Europeans are, and as little able to influence them, except from the greater sympathy with their ways of thinking which previous acquaintance gives. Christianity accordingly cannot come before the Hindus in those aspects which would help most to commend it; it can spread only from individual to individual, without gaining in any of them a centre of power; it draws many out of Hindu society, but cannot be professed by any within it. Thus has caste fortified Hinduism against Christianity with the triple wall of antipathy, terrorism, and isolation.

Points seemingly favourable to Hinduism.

Such then are the points of resemblance and the points of antagonism between the two religions, and it might well seem that the latter are so strong as to prevent our having much hope from the former. But the very strength of the moral contrast between the two should strengthen the desire of all, who have felt the beneficent influence of Christianity, to extend its benefits to the Hindus. There are, however, certain facts which seem to militate against this view of the moral character of the two systems, and to show that practically the difference is not so great. These are the degraded character of many in Christian lands, and the excellent character and high social virtue of many of the Hindus. But a close examination of these facts will show that they have not a direct bearing on the question in hand.

Degraded condition of many Christians.

It may be granted that the lower orders of the Hindus are no worse than the lapsed masses of Great Britain, that the vices and crimes of the one are just as bad as the vices and crimes of the other. But, in comparing the lapsed masses of this country with the worst castes of Hindus, it must be remembered that the defect in the former is their irreligion, in the latter it is their religion. With the former the religious faculty is either dormant or deadened, with the latter it is in full exercise. No Englishman, of whatever social status, thinks of justifying any form of vice or crime on the grounds of religion. Those who do practise thefts or violence, who commit robbery or murder, who indulge in drunkenness or uncleanness, never think of associating these acts with the Christian religion. They are either ignorant of what that religion is, or it has lost its power over them, and they know they are acting in opposition to it. But let the religious faculty be awakened and enlightened by Christian teaching, let it assert its power over them, and they will cease to perform such acts. Now, a Hindu will commit all these crimes, believing that in committing them he is not only not offending against religion, but even performing religious acts. It was as a religious act that the Thug murdered his victims, that the father killed his new-born infant daughter, that the son applied the torch to the pile of wood on to which his mother had mounted. Uncleanness is as much a part of Hindu worship as it was of the heathen worship in Corinth and Ephesus in the days of the Apostle Paul. There is scarcely a crime which Hinduism will not allow in some men, because it is a caste practice. The lapsed masses, then, in the large cities of Great Britain are low and degraded because they are not Christians. The masses of India are low and degraded because they are Hindus. The former are fallen in spite of, the latter in consequence of, their religion. The same may be said in comparing the lives of many professed Christians with the lives of many professed Hindus. The inconsistencies of the former are the consistencies of the latter. This may be a strong argument for seeking to give Christianity a stronger and wider hold on the mass of Englishmen, but it is no argument for withholding it from India.

The good men among Hindus and Christians.

But, it is further contended, there are good men among the Hindus as well as among Christians, persons who teach a pure morality and who practise it, and we must judge of a religion by the best examples it produces, not by the worst. Again, it must here be decided whether what is good in these examples is the fruit of their religion or not. John Stuart Mill was a fine specimen of a man and a philosopher, but his excellences were in no way due to Christian teaching, and Christianity must point for examples of its effects to other instances. So too we must judge whether what is good in any Hindu is a special result of Hinduism or of naturally good principles, and whether what is good in them can influence their countrymen,—whether Hinduism can become a *power* for good. That it includes much that is good, and that it recognises good, I have sought to show. There are some who dwell more especially on this side of it, and those who do so may find in its literature much to encourage them and stimulate them. But that it also recognises the bad, and that those who wish to follow evil may also find in its sacred books much to encourage them, is also true. Hinduism does not discourage good, except in so far as it does not discourage evil; but that is quite sufficient to prevent it being a power for good.

CHAPTER II.

RELIGIOUS REFORM IN INDIA.

HINDUISM as it is cannot be a moral power. But may not the evil be so eliminated that the good only will remain? May Hinduism not be so reformed as to make it a power for good? This point demands consideration, for it is the point to which the controversy has practically come. No Hindus who seek to maintain the friendly recognition of European thinkers will maintain that Hinduism as it was, or even Hinduism as it is, can continue in India; they have, therefore, set themselves to attempt its reformation, and make it worthy of the civilization of the nineteenth century. Can Hinduism be reformed?

What, then, is the smallest change that will effect this reformation and make Hinduism a power for progress and improvement? It What change will reform Hinduism?

can be nothing less than making good an essential instead of an accident. But this cannot be done on the basis of pantheism. Without belief in a personal, holy God there can be no religious belief in the universal obligation to do good and to shun evil. Thus, unless theism be substituted for pantheism, obligation to seek virtue and to shun vice for freedom from virtue as from vice, Hinduism cannot be reformed. That is to say, unless Hinduism cease to be Hinduism, it cannot be reformed.

Holiness destructive of Hinduism.

Introduce into Hinduism the element of perfect holiness on the part of God, and corresponding moral obligation on the part of man, and which of its doctrines or institutions can stand? Its conception of the Supreme Lord, or Supreme Spirit, is at once destroyed, for it makes him as free from hatred of sin as from love of sin. Its whole pantheon of gods and goddesses, made from his parts, is swept away into the limbo of thieves and liars, of adulterers and murderers. Its worship becomes an empty form, if not an abomination; its holy men shameless beggars and impostors. Even its supreme ordinance, the law of caste, must perish. When the Hindus have learned that falsehood is to be shunned more than contact with a sweeper, dishonesty more than allowing the shadow of a European to fall on their hearth while their food is being cooked, uncleanness more than receiving food from one of another tribe or trade, the days of caste are numbered. What remains? Vicarious suffering for sin, the incarnation of God, man striving to be like God. But that vicarious suffering will be a free, personal, conscious act, not an inevitable, blind, unconscious fate; that incarnation will be one, and not many—holy, and not sinful—Christ, and not Krishna; that striving to be like God will be a striving to make our humanity holy as He is, not to dry up and annihilate our humanity altogether. These are, however, marks of the religion of the Bible, not of the religion of the Puranas. Christianity is the only possible reformation of Hinduism that can make it a power for reforming and elevating man.

Where Hindus have tried religious reform Hindu Reformers.

without Christianity one of two results has followed:—either, quitting Hinduism, they have gone further from it than even Christianity; or, trying to remain within Hinduism, they have sunk back into its powerless quietism. This we see exemplified in the history of the Brahma Samàj of Calcutta. This society or church owes its origin to the well-known Ram Mohun Roy, who, towards the beginning of this century, tried to lead his countrymen to a better faith. By his publication of the 'Precepts of Jesus,' he showed whence he had himself derived his inspiration, and what he looked on as the best guide to life, but he was ready to select also from what he considered good in the Hindu scriptures, especially the Vedas. He did not form a sect or establish a mode of worship, but the Samàj was established in 1830, three years before his death, by those who had imbibed his opinions. About ten years thereafter Babu Debendra Nath Tagore became one of its leaders, and under him it made considerable progress towards separation from orthodox Hinduism; but he could not break

Brahma Samàj.

off from it altogether. This step was taken by Babu Keshub Chunder Sen, who joined the Samàj in 1857, and soon became a leader. He was much more progressive than his colleagues, and in 1865 brought matters to a crisis by demanding, among other things, that the external signs of caste distinction should be no longer used. When this was refused by the majority, Keshub Chunder Sen formed the 'Brahma Samàj of India,' called also the progressive Brahmists, while the others remained as the Adi or original Samàj.

The creed of Chunder Sen and his party is simple,—the fatherhood of God and the brotherhood of man. He looks for its enforcement to the Scriptures of all creeds, and selects what is best in them for instruction and for worship. His high character, the strong moral tone of his teaching, and his zealous labours for the diffusion of knowledge, point him out as one of the likeliest of Indian reformers. His principles too, as being hostile to pantheism, idolatry, and caste, must command the sympathy of all who desire the The progressive Brahmists.

enlightenment of India. But his system is not Hinduism, nor is it Indian in anything but name. It is more un-Hindu than Christianity. It is the Spiritualism of Newman and Parker, and it ignores those true religious aspirations in Hinduism, which Christianity recognises, and for which it offers satisfaction. A divine revelation, a divine incarnation, and vicarious atonement for sin, are elements which bring Christianity nearer than Brahmöism to the faith of the Hindus, and make it more likely to be ultimately the refuge of those who feel that the old faith does not satisfy their religious wants. Chunder Sen's movement is too recent for us yet to predict what the verdict of his countrymen may be, but meanwhile Christianity can claim that, in so far as nationality or adaptability to the Hindus is concerned, it is a better instrument of reformation than Brahmöism. This has shown that it is impossible to leave Hinduism, and not accept Christianity, without going further from it than even Christianity does.

Defects of their system.

But already the fatal defects of the system are beginning to be apparent. It is failing in the struggle with Hinduism, and it is failing to maintain a consistent position itself. 'There is something in Pantheism so deep, that naught in bare Deism can meet it. Deism is not so deep. And Pantheism may well keep the house till a stronger than Deism comes to take possession of it. In Jesus Christ I find the only true solution of the mystery.'[1] These words of one of our deepest thinkers are finding practical illustration in the history of the present attempted theistic reformation of Hinduism. Brahmöism wins more converts from the educated classes than Christianity does, but it fails to retain them. They cannot find in the system anything to compensate for the loss occasioned by being out-casted, nor anything which they cannot believe as well within their caste, and so numbers of them seek re-admission to caste privileges. Christianity wins fewer converts from among the educated, but it retains them all. The tenets of the Samàj are also keenly assailed by the native Christians, especially on the question of the expiation of sin. When

[1] Duncan, *Horæ Peripateticæ.*

pressed, its advocates can present no better solution than that which is the starting-point of Hinduism, and they seem to have entered on ground which will bring them back to the old Hindu solution of metempsychosis.[2]

Course of the Adi Samàj.

And what has been the course of the residue—of those who formed the Adi Samàj, and tried to reform Hinduism by remaining within its pale? Their avowed object was to make the new religion a fulfilment of the old faith instead of an abrogation of it. The texts they compiled were taken only from

[2] 'In a letter to the *Mirror*, the well-known native Christian scholar, Professor Ram Chandra, now of Putiala, exposes the Brahmo idea of sin as that which exhausts itself and leaves men holy, adding: "The religious belief of the Brahmos is as contrary to the will of God as Atheism, and it is a blasphemy to call it by the name of *Theism*, it being worse than Atheism; for while Atheism promises utter annihilation after death, and thus only destroys the fear of punishment hereafter, Brahmoism gladdens the hearts of all those who live and glory in sin in this world with the certain hope of everlasting life and joy in the next." The *Mirror's* reply shirks the question: "His logic is wrong, and his heart seems unkind and unable to realize the fulness of Divine love. Theism of all systems of faith offers the greatest discouragement to sin, because it holds that Christians, Hindus, and Brahmos will all be adequately punished for their sins, here or hereafter, and that no form of expiation can secure the remission of such punishment."'—*Friend of India*, June 1874.

the Hindu Shastras, and they allowed what they termed innocent Hindu usages and customs to remain. It was, in fact, an attempt to found a system of Deism on a system of pantheistic idolatry—a task much more hopeless than to exterminate the latter. They taught one personal God, but to denominate Him they adopted the formula of Vedantic pantheism—one only, without a second.[3] They denounced idolatry, but allowed it on certain occasions and in certain circumstances. How long such a system might have continued in other circumstances it is impossible to say, but, exposed as it is to the assaults of progressive Brahmöism and of Christianity, it has been obliged to fall back further and further on its original source, and is now scarcely to be distinguished from orthodox Hinduism. When one of its leaders, Rajnarayan Bose, could defend Hinduism as superior to Christianity and other religions, not although it maintains, but[4] because it maintains, inferior

Its relapse into Orthodox Hinduism.

[3] See *ante*, p. 94.

[4] In a lecture on the Superiority of Hinduism to Christianity,

stages of religious belief in its own bosom—these inferior stages including the worship of Krishna, and of the linga, the sensuality of the Maharajas, and the self-torture of the yogis; not although it grasps, but because it grasps within its embrace all human knowledge, though that knowledge, as taught in the Shastras, includes a geography with oceans of curds and continents of sugar surrounding a top-shaped mountain 800,000 miles high—he had evidently begun to lose sight of the nature of true religion. The next step soon followed: when challenged by an esteemed missionary in Calcutta for admitting the Tantras as sacred books, he defends himself thus:—

'Though they are not reckoned as religious authorities

---

delivered by Bose in Calcutta in 1872, and reported in the *Friend of India*, the following are two of the twelve merits of Hinduism adduced:—

'IX. That Hinduism maintains inferior stages of religious belief in its own bosom, in harmony with the nature of man, who cannot but pass through several stages of religious development before being able to grasp the Supreme Being.

'XI. That the Hindu religion is of a very comprehensive character, as grasping within its embrace all human knowledge, all civil polity, and all domestic economy, impenetrating every concern of human life with the sublime influence of religion.'

so much in other parts of India as in Bengal, and contain many indecent passages, and therefore occupy the lowest rank among the Shastras even in Bengal, they, especially the Mahanirvana Tantra, contain some of the sublimest precepts of morality and religion. The incongruity may appear strange to us, but still such is the case. Though some Tantras enjoin excessive drinking and unlawful intercourse, there are others which deprecate them in the strongest terms.' [5]

Here we see the position to which Adi Brahmöism has been brought—the old slough of Hinduism, utterly impotent for any good. The Tantras are sacred books, because they contain some sublime precepts of morality and religion, and these the Adi Brahmists accept and seek to follow; but they also enjoin excessive drinking and unlawful intercourse; and these passages the Sàktas accept and carry into practice. Both are founded on the Shastras, and both are included within the pale of Hinduism; and this, Rajnarayan Bose considers, shows the superiority of Hinduism to Christianity. It is not surprising that their original leader, the sincere and earnest Debendra Nath Tagore, should have sought refuge from this position in as-

[5] *Friend of India*, 1872.

ceticism, trying to spend his days as he thinks the great Rishis or saints of old may have spent theirs, among the Himalayas.[6]

Christianity the only reformation of Hinduism.

I write this in no spirit of triumph or exultation over the Adi Brahmists, but from a deep conviction that no reform attempted on the basis of Hinduism can be permanent. Hinduism is essentially quiescent: it tolerates everything but change, and forbids the attacking even of what is false, as intolerance and bigotry. Adi Brahmöism set out with the design of fulfilling the old religion, and it has done so; but it has proved that no fulfilment of the old religion can be a reformation. This can be accomplished only by fulfilling what is good, and rejecting, opposing, denouncing what is evil—the principles of Christianity, not of Hinduism. Already Christianity has won some among the Hindus, who accept it as the fulfilment of what is best in the old religion of India, and whose patriotism receives thereby an elevation and intensity such as is not attained to by their heathen fellow-countrymen.

[6] *Bombay Guardian*, Nov. 24, 1873.

'That our Aryan ancestors did to an appreciable extent comprehend the true meaning of sacrifice, and had brought to India certain traditions of that primitive Revelation, cannot be doubted; and, in enforcing the Gospel of Him who came to fulfil the law and the prophets, it is necessary to guard against the rude assaults on the relics of that Revelation which may be traced in the country. The Gospel preached to the Hindus should be in adaptation to those relics *as much* as the integrity of the Truth will allow, and not *as little* as human ignorance or caprice will tolerate. The former policy of action will conduce to the service of God and Truth, the latter to that of human practices and corporations, however excellent they may be. . . . He would be a sorry preacher of Christ indeed who would act the part of a Vandal to such texts as these,[7] instead of presenting the Saviour as their fulfiller and accomplisher, whom indeed their authors may be held to have fervently desired to see, but could not.'[8]

This is the language of a Christian Hindu patriot, appealing to what is best in the old religion and literature of his nation as neither a Vaishnava nor a Saiva, neither an Adi Brahmist nor a progressive Brahmist could.

Other causes of decay in Hinduism.

I believe, then, that the history of all attempts at reformation that have been made on the basis of Hinduism shows that no permanent result can be looked for from them. It must also be borne in mind that there are

[7] See *ante*, p. 41. [8] *Bengal Christian Herald*, Feb. 1874.

disintegrating processes at work in India which must ultimately destroy the old religion of the country. To mention nothing else, the system of secular education introduced by the British Government has this tendency. Hinduism cannot stand before the culture of the nineteenth century, and those who make any progress in acquaintance with modern literature, science, and philosophy find them incompatible with the faith in which they have been born. But Government education cannot supply anything in place of that which it destroys. Of the effect which it is having on the Hindus I will again let a Hindu speak:—

'Up to the time of his passing the entrance examination of the Calcutta University, he (young Bengal) remains a Hindu of more or less degree of orthodoxy. When he crosses that Rubicon, Hinduism gradually slackens its grasp of him. He now tampers with Deism. He loses all faith in the religion of his ancestors. He does not inquire into Christianity, taking it for granted that it is a system of superstition. Mahommedanism he hates with a perfect hatred. Deism relaxes its hold upon him till he runs adrift upon the rocks of unbelief, and by the time he has become a graduate of the University he ceases to believe in anything. A few become Brahmos, fewer still

Christians, but the vast bulk are left stranded on the shoals of scepticism.'[9]

Dangers of mere secular education.

This is indeed true as yet of only a very limited number—those who have passed through the university curriculum. They, however, come more prominently before the English public, and are apt to be taken as types of all Hindus. Hence a mistaken notion is gaining ground that Hinduism is altogether a thing of the past, and has no hold on the Hindus, or, at all events, the educated Hindus. But it is true only of some of those who have received a university education—possibly about one ten-thousandth part of the whole population. Hinduism is still a living faith with a hundred and forty millions of our fellow-subjects. The system I have described is still 'the strong man that keeps the house' which Christianity is seeking to enter. But English education and European culture have only begun their work. They must increase and spread, and ultimately leaven the whole people; and if they be left to work alone the above extracts describe

[9] *Bengal Magazine.*

pretty well what the result will be. It is a 'religious reform' that may be contemplated with satisfaction by Comptists and materialists; but it is surely a fate from which it is worth while for Christians to seek to rescue India. It is a duty which they owe to their Master as well as to the Hindus, to show these that the material progress and scientific enlightenment which are destroying their old faiths and dethroning their old gods, do not imply the renunciation of all faith, the abandonment of all belief in divine power; that they may consist with a faith which fulfils the longing of man's nature, and draws him to holiness infinitely more powerfully than that faith which they destroy.

CHAPTER III.

ATTITUDE OF CHRISTIANITY WITH REGARD TO HINDUISM.

THE review which we have taken of the relative positions of Hinduism and Christianity must make all Christians feel the responsibility that lies on them to press on the Hindus the acceptance of Christ, and we now come to consider the attitude which the Church should take in order to insure success. I will here dwell on only two principles that must guide it, and that are being somewhat lost sight of—Intolerance and Confidence.

Christian tolerance and intolerance.

I use purposely the word intolerance, for it is with this that the Hindus reproach Christianity, and it virtually amounts to love of truth. If Christianity once becomes tolerant, as they understand the word, it falls vanquished—it becomes Hinduism. While friendly to the Hindus it must be intolerant of their errors. To the false tolerance of Hinduism it opposes a true intolerance, to the false intolerance of Hinduism it opposes a true tolerance. To that tolerance, which admits as true every form of belief held by others, however much opposed to that held by one's-self—which allows every kind of worship and every mode of life to be equally acceptable to God and equally conducive to salvation,—it opposes the intolerance of declaring the consistency of truth, and the universal obligation on all to search it out and act according to it—to seek to know God's will and to live according to it. To the false intolerance which forbids a man liberty to change his creed and act out his convictions, it opposes the tolerance of allowing, nay requiring, every man to profess what he believes to be true, and to act out his belief, provided that that does not include practices opposed to morality.

Intolerance necessary to the success of Christianity.

Gibbon assigns the intolerance of the early Christians as one of the principal secondary causes of the rapid spread of Christianity in the first two centuries. The Greeks and

Romans were quite willing to admit Christ into their pantheon as one of their gods, and to allow worship to be paid to Him along with others. But this concession the early Christians refused; they insisted that He alone was God, and that the others were no gods—that He alone should be worshipped, and that the worship of the others was a sin abominable in His sight. Had they taken up any more tolerant position than this, the mission of Christianity would have failed. By holding true to this principle they ultimately overthrew the paganism of the Roman world. And it is only by a similar intolerance that Christianity can be successful in India. The position of Hinduism is indeed much more subtle and dangerous than that of ancient paganism. The Hindu pundit does not say Christ may be worshipped as well as Vishnu. He says Christ is Vishnu; he whom you worship under the name of Christ is the same whom I worship under the name of Vishnu; you worship him after your fashion and I worship him after my fashion. In taking this position, the Hindu considers he occupies a position far superior to the Christian ; and there are not wanting philosophers, or persons who consider themselves philosophers, in this country, who take the same view of the matter, who contrast the broad charity of the Hindu advocate with the narrow bigotry of the Christian advocate—the clear vision of the former enabling him to rise to the conception of the one God, whom all nations on the face of the whole earth adore, under whatever name, while the limited, shortsighted range of the latter prevents him taking in anything but the one form to which he has been accustomed. But observe the consequence that follows. If Christ and Vishnu are one and the same, then Christ and Krishna are also one and the same—the holy, harmless, undefiled Prophet of Galilee the same as the clever thief of Brindaban and the adulterous lover of the gopis ; He who came not to be ministered unto, but to minister, the same as he who spent his time in luxurious ease at Dwarka, with his sixteen thousand one hundred and eight wives. Both are equally manifestations of the same God, the example of both equally binding.

Popular Hindu toleration of Christianity.

The Hindus thus do not propose to admit Christ to their pantheon as did the ancient Romans; they say that He is there already, under the name of their own god. And the blinding, debasing influence of their system appears in their not being able to behold any incongruity between these manifestations, or the impossibility of both being ways of salvation. Recurring to the image of water, which I have already given,[1] and which is a favourite one with them, they will say Christ is the river by which Christians reach the ocean of liberation, and Krishna the river by which the Hindus reach it. They acknowledge the moral superiority of Jesus. I never had difficulty in getting Hindus to acknowledge that Christ was a holy, sinless, perfect being, and Krishna a sinful, vile, abominable character; but then I was no nearer gaining my end than before. They would reply, though that is the case, we can gain our end

[1] See *ante*, p. 106.

as well through him as you do through Christ, a drop of water will reach the ocean in a muddy stream as well as in a pure stream.

Duty of the Church.

Enough has been said to show the extremely subtle and dangerous position which Hinduism takes up with regard to Christianity, and the great necessity that exists for the latter to maintain an uncompromising, unyielding position with regard to it. The work of the Church then is plain—to hold, without flinching, without yielding one iota, the old message of the apostles, 'Neither is there salvation in any other; for there is none other *Name* under heaven given among men whereby we must be saved.'[2] While gladly welcoming all the truth that is in Hinduism, there must be no parleying with the great falsehood that characterizes that system; while recognising the attempts that it has made to supply the wants of the human heart with the objects they desire, there must be no consenting to the false as the true object; while gladly tracing all relics of a true primitive revelation and religion

[2] Acts iv. 12.

that Hinduism may have preserved, there must be a clear distinction between them and the perversions and accretions of human invention that have so entirely covered them. Only by a bold, unwavering maintenance and propagation of the truth can Christianity hope to triumph. This is alike its duty and its safety. If nothing else, the fate of its great rival Mahommedanism in India should be a warning to it against a false charity and a false liberality.

Confidence in the success of preaching and teaching.

While the Church should prosecute the work of evangelizing India with a spirit of true friendly intolerance, it should also carry to it a spirit of confidence, inspired alike by the means at its disposal and the past success of its efforts. What are the means at its disposal,—what are 'the weapons of our warfare?' If anything is to be learned from the past history of religion in India, it is that those appointed—preaching and teaching—are the best. Mahommedanism, trying force and the sword, failed to gain any large portion of the Hindus; and these were the most worthless of the Hindus, and became the most worthless of the Mahommedans. Buddhism tried nothing but persuasion, and in a short time spread all over India. It failed indeed to secure its conquests from causes which we have already considered, and which Christianity will guard against; but the splendid fact remains that, by preaching, it spread its way all over India, while its successor, trying the sword, utterly failed. This is an encouraging fact for Christianity, because we may hope that the means which were successful once will be successful again.

Attitude of Government.

To this method of propagandism Christianity has hitherto confined itself in India. It has had the power of the sword there for upwards of a hundred years, but it has never degraded itself by using that for its own advancement. It may be said that the Government there is purely a political and not a religious power, and that is true; but it is also true that, at the head of the Government, there have been men of high religious principle, and these have carefully avoided doing anything to interfere with the religious convictions of those whom they governed. The declaration of the Queen in her proclamation assuming the government of India,—'Firmly relying ourselves on the truth of Christianity, and acknowledging with gratitude the solace of religion, we disclaim alike the right and the desire to impose our convictions on any of our subjects,'—shows the true position of a Christian government.

Government interference has rather strengthened Hinduism.

It was indeed impossible for such a government to abstain from all interference with some of the religious practices which were found in India. The burning of the widow on her husband's funeral pyre, the custom of female infanticide, the immolation of human victims before the wheels of Juggernauth's car, were all defended on the ground that they were religious ordinances; and were all repressed with a firm hand by a Christian government. But this has had the effect of strengthening Hinduism by forcing it practically to be more in accordance with the laws of natural religion. The rising generation of Hindus have almost forgotten that sati, thuggism, female infanticide, and human sacrifice, were once parts of their religion, and they are learning to speak of them with a horror scarcely less than that which Christians feel for such cruelties. Thus has the very action of Christianity in India helped to strengthen its rival, by forcing it out of some of those positions which weakened it. The contest is now one between ultimate principles, maintained solely by persuasion on the one side, and by persuasion allied with social terrorism on the other.

Difficulties in employment of the means.

In estimating the past success or future prospects of the contest, we must not forget the immediate disadvantage under which the employment of these means has laid Christianity, and the special difficulties it has had to encounter. Christianity has not come before the Hindus in the way most likely to attract them. It has been spread indeed only by preaching and teaching, but the preaching has not been of the kind most fitted to impress the natives of India. The

Christianity not ascetic.

Buddhist preachers were ascetics; they renounced family life and all worldly ties in order to spread their faith, and the people flocked to them in multitudes. Every founder of a reforming sect in Hinduism has taken the same course, and thereby obtained a reputation for sanctity, and drawn a large number of disciples. If Christian missionaries were to become ascetics likewise, to clothe themselves in the coarsest of rags, and shun all but the coarsest of food or what might be given them by their disciples, if they were to travel barefoot from place to place, measuring the length of the way by prostrations of the body, they might soon number their converts by millions instead of thousands. But this would be to spread Christianity by renouncing it,—to foster in the minds of the Hindus the conviction that in it, as in their own religion, there was a distinction between the holy man and the family man, between the man of business and the man of piety, that no one while discharging the ordinary duties of life could be a Christian in the highest sense of the word; instead of showing them that religion directs and sanctifies every relation of life, that the whole life should be a worship of God, that there is no order of priesthood but in the sense in which every Christian is a priest, Christianity must come before them as a religion of daily life attainable by all and by all alike. This will ultimately prove its strength in India as elsewhere, but meanwhile it hinders its acceptance with the Hindus, for it is an idea new to them.

Christians excluded from social intercourse.

Not only is the idea different from what they are accustomed to, but the social organization of the Hindus makes it doubly difficult for such a religion to be brought before them. I have already shown how caste prevents social intercourse with those of another race and of another creed. The result is, that it prevents Christianity coming before the Hindus in its social aspect; they can judge it only from its external aspect, from its teaching, and not from the view of its influence on daily life. Christianity is also for the Hindus a religion of foreigners, and all their patriotic sentiments lead them to oppose it.

Christianity opposed to Hindu patriotism.

Patriotism as a political power does not exist among the Hindus. For attachment to country their religion has substituted attachment to caste; but this very fact gives their religion a greater significance for them. As with the Jews, so with the Hindus, it is their only symbol of nationality, and while it remains, they care little that they have no political existence. They look to it as the Swiss to their mountains and the English to the sea, as the bulwark of their nation, in which they have never been vanquished, in which they are as much superior to their conquerors as their conquerors are to them in material force—as the vantage-ground from which they can look down on them as unclean cow-eaters. Nor must it be forgotten that the lives of Europeans in India have been a serious obstacle in the way of the spread of Christianity. The native cannot draw a distinction between those who are true in their profession and those who are not; for them all Europeans are Christians, and their lives are the evidence of the practical effects of their faith. Unhappily their lives are too often but little in accordance with the teaching of the gospel, and do not testify to the heathen its moral

Lives of Europeans in India.

superiority over the teaching of their own sacred books.

Christian sects.

Again, the sectarian form in which Christianity has been introduced is a stumbling-block with many, who have become somewhat acquainted with its principles. The various missionary societies in India,—with one exception, which, claiming to be the most catholic, is the most narrowly sectarian,—have agreed to sink their distinctive tenets in presence of a common foe; to avoid occupying the same ground, except in the large centres of population; not to interfere with one another's work, and as far as possible to exhibit the unity instead of the diversities of Christianity. Yet these last cannot but be noticed by the natives, and the different forms of worship and sacrament, the various creeds and formulæ that have been imported to India, European growths on Christianity rather than Christianity itself, have been to it a source of the greatest weakness. Hindus who have learned something of its principles, and been well disposed towards it, have stumbled on this. Christ indicated the oneness and love of His disciples as evidence to the world of their discipleship, and when these are replaced by diversities and jealousies, it is not to be wondered at that the heathen should be repelled from accepting Him.

Christianity a persecuted religion.

Lastly, it must be borne in mind, as a consequence of these obstacles that I have named, that Christianity is in India a persecuted religion. It has not indeed to endure the persecution of the prison and the sword, which tends to give strength and life to the Church, when it has taken firm root in any land, as in Madagascar. The complete fairness and neutrality of the supreme government prevent this, and secure to every one the free profession of his own belief. But there is the social terrorism and persecution of caste, tenfold more difficult to endure, and more deleterious in its effects, and against which no power on earth has yet been able to devise a remedy. It neither confers on its victim the dignity of martyrdom, nor does it call out the stronger and manlier qualities of human nature. It makes its victim an object of reproach and shame, a byword and a disgrace to his kindred, an outcast from family and friends. It pronounces an inexorable ban sufficient to daunt and keep back all, except those whose convictions of the truth and trust in God enable them to rise above all that man generally prizes most.

Rise of a native Christian Church in India.

Taking into account all these hindrances, the introduction of Christianity into India seems about as hopeless a task as can well be imagined; but the best evidence that it is not hopeless is that a Christian Church has already been established there. In 1871 the number of native Christians in India was 224,258,[3] having increased one hun-

[3] The following are the statistics of the Native Protestant Church of India since 1851, when a census was first taken :—

	Foreign Missionaries.	Native Ordained Agents.	Native Christians.	Increase during Decade.
1851	339	21	91,092	
1861	479	97	138,731	47,639, or 52 per cent.
1871	488	225	224,258	85,527, or 61 per cent.

It will be observed that the percentage of increase during the second decade is higher than during the first, though it is on a larger number. The increase in the number of foreign missionaries during that period is only nine, while the increase of native ministers is 128. With regard to the character of the

dred and forty per cent. in twenty years. The very existence of such a body diminishes, and as it increases in numbers and influence will completely remove, many of the adventitious difficulties with which Christianity has hitherto had to contend in India. Social persecution will lose much of its terror when it is shared by a community large enough to protect its own interests. If caste does forbid the commingling of Hindu Christians with those who still remain in the religion of their fathers, they are yet much nearer them than are the English, mingle more with them, understand them better, and have a better opportunity of commending Christianity to them. The native Christians of India have no doubt many defects, yet they are by their lives better

Character of the Native Church.

Native Church the only test which statistics can supply is the proportion of communicants. These numbered

In 1851	14,661,	or 16 per cent. of the total number.
„ 1861	24,976,	„ 18 „ „ „
„ 1871	52,816,	„ 28 „ „ „

The amount raised by Native Christians in 1871 was £8473. Since then two new missions have been established by them. —*Report of Allahabad Conference.*

exponents of Christianity than the majority of the English in India. Their faults and vices are the faults and vices of their countrymen, and these Christianity does not eradicate in a day. Thus it may well happen that a Hindu, even after he has professed faith in Christ, and proved his sincerity by passing through the terrible ordeal which such a profession involves, will be found inferior in reliability, truthfulness and manliness to an Englishman who makes no such profession, but who has from his infancy, by precept, example and the influence of public opinion, been trained in these virtues. But his faith will ultimately produce a marked change in his character, and raise that of the whole community. Already the Indian Church has produced many noble instances of the power of Christianity, and has been adorned by preachers and scholars, who show what the Hindu intellect may accomplish when it is disciplined by Christianity. Some of their works on the religion of their country may claim a place alongside of the best productions of European writers on the same subject.[4]

Another advantage that is gained by the formation of a church, led by such men, is that it removes the charge of Christianity being a foreign faith. Christianity is no more an English religion than it is an Indian religion, but it has hitherto come before the Hindu as such, and only when a powerful native church has been developed will it cease to appear in that form. There can be no doubt that Christianity will assume in India—must indeed assume if it is to be universally triumphant—an Indian form. If the religion of Christ is a world's religion, it must be capable of assuming the form best suited for each nation of the world. It is absurd to suppose that a race which has shown so strong an individuality, especially so

Christianity not a foreign faith.

[4] Among these, there are two works on Hindu Philosophy available to English readers—both by converted Brahmans. One—*Dialogues on Hindu Philosophy*, by the Rev. K. M. Bannerjea (Trübner & Co.)—is written by the author himself in English that will bear comparison with that of the best English writers. The other—*Refutation of Hindu Philosophy*, by Nehemiah Nilkanth—was written in Hindi, and has had the honour of being translated by Dr. Fitz-Edward Hall.

strong a religious individuality, as the Hindus, can, in adopting Christianity, follow closely the European models. To suppose so would be tacitly to allow that Christianity was a European, not a cosmopolitan religion. The countrymen of Buddha and Kapila, of Sankara and Ramanuja, may be trusted in following Christ to follow Him directly, and not merely as interpreted by their European teachers—to say to the latter we will follow you only in so far as you are followers of Christ. That they are already beginning to do so, that they are beginning to take an independent and distinct position, is one of the best proofs that can be given that Christianity may be the religion of India, and the Christian Church a rallying centre of Hindu patriotism.

Characteristics of Indian Christianity.

In nothing is the distinctive character of Indian Christianity making itself more felt than in its utter impatience of all sectarianism and sectarian formulæ. European missionaries in India, as I have said, regret these, and endeavour to keep them in the background as much as possible. But trained up as they are in them, closely connected with powerful ecclesiastical organizations at home, whose history and position make their symbols indispensable, they have not been able to abandon them. But to Hindu Christians they are an abomination, a source of weakness and reproach in the presence of a powerful foe. Both in Culcutta and Bombay, setting aside the distinctive articles of the churches represented there, they are banding themselves together in Catholic associations, and they are showing their purpose and life by establishing undenominational missions among their heathen fellow-countrymen. This is the most hopeful outcome of Indian missions yet. These associations will be the germs of the future Church of India, and will give to it its distinctive character. That it can be creedless is impossible, but its creed will be a definition of Christianity against the foes it has actually to fight, against Hinduism and Mahommedanism, not against European speculations and errors that have been slain centuries ago. In such a result the Churches of Great Britain and

America should rejoice. There is abundance of work for them yet, and there will be for many years to come a need for them to have their missionary societies carried on under their distinctive organizations. But if their object be to introduce to India, not a distinctive form of worship, or system of church government, but Christianity, they will rejoice to see a church developing there which will take the work out of their hands, and by aiding which they may best promote the great end which they have in view.

Encouragements to prosecute the evangelization of India.

Looking forward to this, there is a call to all Christians of Great Britain and America to do more for India than they have done. Five hundred missionaries, even backed as they are by two hundred native agents, are scarcely adequate to produce an impression on upwards of two hundred millions of people. Had they been obliged in despair to abandon the enterprise of converting that nation to Christ, it would have been a result not to be wondered at. Instead of this, what do we find,—a native church already numbering upwards of two hundred thousand, only one to a thousand Hindus indeed, but doubling itself in fifteen years,—a rate of progress which, if continued, would make India Christian within two centuries,—less time than it took to make it Buddhist;—and that church is showing a vitality which proves that it will continue to exist even if it be cut off from the support of Christian nations; that it will be triumphant if these do their duty by it. If ever there was a time when the churches of Great Britain were encouraged by past experience and present prospects to strain every nerve to win India for Christ, the present is that time. Difficulties and hindrances, though still great and many, are surely disappearing. Those principles of human nature which Hinduism has ignored are surely asserting their sway to its overthrow, and the past religious history of India points to Christ as its only possible completion.

Hinduism opposed to human nature.

These principles are consciousness and conscience. The former bears witness to our own personality, the latter to the paramount claims of what is good. Man does not remember ever having been born before, and refuses to accept a responsibility for what he cannot remember having done. The pundits do indeed speak of the delusion which *maya* has thrown over man's spirit, but this is only a flimsy shield to protect their theory from the constantly recurring attacks of man's own consciousness. It can be effective only so long as he chooses to accept the dictum of others on a point on which his own experience is quite as much entitled to credit. In like manner, however philosophy may teach superiority or indifference to good and evil as the summit of human attainment,—however priests may exhibit monsters defiled by every sin as mediums to the winning of final bliss, the conscience which the true God has implanted in man bears testimony to His displeasure against sin, and His delight in holiness. These two great principles still do exist in the Hindus,—antidotes to the subtle pantheistic poison which has for ages been circulating through their national life. These are the auxiliaries to which we have resort in pressing on them the religion of Jesus. In recalling them to their manhood we are calling them to Christianity.

The history of Hinduism a search for Christ.

The past religious history of the Hindus, too, points to Christ as its only possible completion. In the history of their very errors we may find encouragement for the future. A dreary history of human darkness has been the search of that great people after God and the truth for three thousand years. Yet let us recognise that it is the truth they have been feeling after. Partial glimpses of it they have had and followed, till they found them unsatisfying for man's whole nature; then they have followed other parts of truth, going from extreme to extreme of religious thought, like a pendulum whose beat is through thousands of years. Impatient of the dead sacerdotalism into which primitive elemental worship and primitive sacrifice had developed, they sought rest first in Buddhism, and again in Hinduism. That offered them morality without God, and that failed to satisfy them; this offers them God without holiness, incarnations without morality, and this too is failing to satisfy them. Christianity offers them Christ,—God and holiness, a perfect incarnation, the desire of the Hindu as of all nations.

APPENDIX.

APPENDIX.

A.

BUDDHA'S SYSTEM.

THE teaching of Buddha may be divided into two parts—Doctrinal and Practical. The former consists of what is known as the 'Law of the Wheel,' or the Four Great Verities which he discovered under the mimosa tree. These are—

1st, Suffering exists wherever animated being exists.

2nd, The cause of suffering is desire, *i.e.* a craving for what is only a temporary illusion.

3rd, Deliverance from suffering can be effected only by deliverance from desire, or by attaining Nirvàna.

4th. Nirvàna can be attained only by following the method of Buddha.

The method included in the fourth verity consists of eight paths leading to Nirvàna. Of these the first four applicable to all are—*1st,* right vision or faith (*cf.* Matt. vi. 22); *2nd,* right judgment or thoughts; *3rd,* right language; *4th,* right actions. This is a simple enough statement, that Buddha's disciples must have the right faith, and seek to be perfect in thought, word, and deed. The remaining four paths are applicable especially to the priesthood, and show the influence of his false conception of man's end, or Nirvàna. They are—*5th,* right means of livelihood, or the profession of a recluse; *6th,* right application of the spirit to the study of the law; *7th,* right memory, or freedom from error in recollecting the law; *8th,* right meditation, which conducts the intelligence to a quietude nearly approaching Nirvàna.

The Practical part of his system has the same double aspect both in its negative and positive injunctions. The negative part has five commandments binding on all: 1*st*, not to kill—extending even to animal life; 2*nd*, not to steal; 3*rd*, not to commit adultery; 4*th*, not to lie—this extends to the using of improper language; 5*th*, not to use strong drink; and five binding specially on priests: 1*st*, not to take repasts at improper times; 2*nd*, not to look at dances and plays; 3*rd*, not to have costly raiments, perfumes, &c.; 4*th*, not to have a large bed or quilt; 5*th*, not to receive gold or silver.

The positive part of the moral law consists in enjoining six virtues on all—Charity, purity, patience, courage, contemplation, science. Of these the first—charity—is the most important, and includes caring not only for man, but also for all animate beings down to the smallest insect. Twelve observances are further enjoined on recluses: 1*st*, to use clothes made only of rags picked up in burying-grounds or on the road; 2*nd*, to have only three such coats all sewn by the wearer's hands; 3*rd*, to have a cloak of yellow wool to cover all, prepared in the same way; 4*th*, to live only on food given in charity and without asking; 5*th*, to take only one meal daily; 6*th*, never to eat or drink after mid-day; 7*th*, to live in the forests or jungles; 8*th*, to have no roof but the foliage of the trees; 9*th*, to sit with the back supported by the trunk of the tree; 10*th*, to sleep sitting and not lying; 11*th*, never to change the position of the carpet or quilt when it has once been spread; 12*th*, to go once a month to burying or burning grounds to meditate on the vanity of earth.[1] These are rules which Buddha is said to have followed himself, and which are enjoined on his disciples.

It will be observed that throughout this teaching there is a complete distinction, if not antagonism, between the religion for the masses and the discipline for the priesthood. The

[1] Abridged from St. Hilaire.

former is intelligible and human, and a clear expression of the moral law as regards human relationship, though defective as ignoring the filial relationship. The latter is a cold-hearted, unnatural endeavour to attain a selfish end. Wheeler, in his *History of India*, notes this antagonism, and conceives it 'incredible that such an enthusiastic philanthropist should have formed the conception of Nirvàna,' and 'that he should have propounded out of his individual consciousness such an artificial system of metaphysical religion as that which is involved in the modern form of Buddhism and enforced in the legend of his own life. Accordingly the suspicion arises that the conception of Nirvàna and the metaphysical dogmas of Buddhism may possibly be more modern developments of the ancient morality which was taught by Sàkya Muni, and that Buddhism was originally a pure and simple faith, which has been strangely perverted by the monastic teachers of a later age.'[2] The author here seems, however, to omit to take into account the influence which Brahmanism must have exercised on Buddha. We can hardly suppose him to have divorced himself from all the thought of his age. He did not follow the Brahmanical system slavishly, but transfused it in his own mind, and produced a system which, however perverted or exaggerated by later teachers, yet laid down the lines on which they have proceeded. It may be granted that his faults were the faults of his age, but we can hardly suppose him to have emancipated himself from them altogether. The intensity of his own convictions led him to make his profession as a recluse subservient to the service of his fellows, but as the spirit died out in his followers the demarcation between the recluse and the laity became complete.

'This line is perpetually slurred over in ancient and modern Buddhism, and yet it finds general expression throughout the Buddhist world. The monks scarcely appear to interfere with the religion of the masses. They teach the boys in the monastery schools, but that is in accordance with their discipline. Occasionally they appear to preach, but it is only

[2] Vol. iii. p. 148.

to recite certain precepts and observances, or certain passages from the life of Buddha, in a kind of chorus. So, too, the laity have little to do with the monks, unless they themselves enter the monastery. They are ever ready with their alms of food and clothing, and ever ready to pay visits of respect and reverence, but this is only a part of their religion. Still, on all occasions there is a genuine and kindly veneration displayed toward the monk, which is rarely exhibited by the people of India toward the arrogant and exclusive Brahman.'[3]

B.

SCHOOLS OF HINDU PHILOSOPHY.

There are said to be six schools or *Darshan* of Hindu Philosophy, but they are arranged also in three pairs according to the views they support.

I. The Sensational School included, 1*st*, the Nyàya or Logic, said to be founded by Gautama. He taught the method of reasoning which has been adopted by all the schools, whence the name of his. He considered Sensation to be the origin of our knowledge, and set himself to investigate it. He started the idea of *Adrishta* the unseen, to account for what cannot be accounted for otherwise.

2*nd*. The Atomic School, said to be founded by Kanada, is connected with the Nyàya. But he supplemented it by investigating the objects of sensation, and introduced the idea of atoms as the material cause of the universe.

II. The second pair included, 1*st*, The Sankhya or numeral system, said to be founded by Kapila. It starts with the object of our perceptions and sensations, and may, therefore, be considered materialistic. It teaches the eternity of matter. God could not create the universe without desire and consequent want of power. If He had desire He could not have power,

---

[3] Wheeler's Hist. of India, vol. iii. p. 152.

and if He had power He could not have desire. According to him Prakriti—which corresponds very much with matter, as explained by the most advanced school of modern materialists,—the rootless root, is the eternal cause of all things, and contains within itself 'the promise and potency' of every form of existence. It is inanimate, non-sentient and prolific. Beside it is Purusha, the soul, intelligent, sentient and non-productive, because free and indifferent.

2nd, The Yoga or mystic system founded by Patanjali: adopted the above system, but introduced the idea of God, and dwelt more on how the soul is to be freed from bondage to Prakriti.

III. The third pair included, 1st, the Purva Mimansa—original decider—founded by Jaimini, which sought to bring back the Brahmans to the Vedas as the source of authority. It has but one distinctive tenet, the eternity of the Vedas, or as he puts it, the eternity of word or sound (Sabda).

2nd, The Uttara Mimansa—second decider—said to be founded by Vyasa. It appeals to the Veda too as decider; but attaches itself to the concluding part of it, the Upanishads (see *ante*, p. 46), and hence is commonly called the Vedanta. It seeks to answer the question what is and what is not, and answers Brahma, God, alone is, everything else is not. One section, acknowledging the reality of the visible universe, identifies it with God; another, the more general, denies the reality of the visible world, and calls it Màyà, or illusion. This is now the most influential school, and the study of the others is supposed to be incomplete without a knowledge of it.

With all the schools two axioms are accepted—*ex nihilo nihil fit*, nothing from nothing; and the transmigration of the soul. Their object is to explain the existence of the world and the circumstances of human life in conformity with these axioms. The authors of the various schools are given here as generally accepted by the Hindus, but there is doubt whether they are real or mythical characters. There is also considerable doubt as to the date of the rise of the various schools. Some make the older ones anterior to Buddhism, but Bannerjea, whom I have followed, advances strong reasons for considering them all subsequent to the rise of that religion and designed to combat it.

C.

HINDU LOGIC.

The form of the Hindu syllogism goes far to illustrate the Hindu mode of reasoning. It consists of five parts.

1*st*, The Proposition (*pratagya*) as :	The mountain is fiery.
2*nd*, The Reason (*hetu*),	Because it gives forth smoke ;
3*rd*, The Example (*Udaharna*),	For whatever is smoky is fiery, as a culinary hearth ;
4*th*, The Application (*Upanaya*),	But so is this mountain smoky :
5*th*, The Conclusion (*Nigaman*),	Therefore it is fiery.

The last three members of this syllogism correspond very much with the Aristotelian, and either the first two or last two seem superfluous. The advocates of Hindu Logic defend it on the ground that it is rhetorical rather than philosophical, designed to convince an adversary, to display a truth already discovered rather than to investigate the truth itself. But this is its great vice. There is no canon for the investigation or discovery of truth. It is obvious that its weakness lies in the third member, the example. If this were always made a true induction or a carefully tested example, it would be legitimate. But it admits of a simple instance establishing a universal conclusion, or the most distant analogy being taken for an instance in point. This is the defect of the syllogism, and it is the defect of all Hindu reasoning. I once asked a pundit to state logically his argument that man's spirit was sinless, which he did as follows :—

Man's spirit is sinless,

Because it is distinct from the sin which man commits ;
For all things are distinct from that which they contain, as the water of a muddy stream is distinct from the mud which it contains ;
But so is the spirit of man distinct from the sin which it may be said to contain :
Therefore it is sinless.

This was an attempt to put into a logical form the stock argument used by the Hindus—Spirit is free from sin as water is distinct from all the dirt which may be mingled with it.

D.

MAHOMMEDAN DOCTRINE OF SIN.

The following extracts from the Mahommedan Commentary on the Holy Bible by Sayad Ahmad, C.S.I., will show the Mahommedan view of sin and its origin :—

'When God created man and gave him life, he was like other animals wholly void of discernment—he had not the power of knowing good and evil. Only in so far as God showed him, did he know anything. For this reason he was without vexation, he was wholly guiltless, and he had no fear of any kind of death, for what he did at that time, he did not with his own understanding. God revealed to him the power of knowing good and evil, and warned him not to take it, for, if he did, he would die a certain kind of death, namely he would fall into this severe calamity, that he would be responsible for his own deeds, would have himself to distinguish between every action as right or wrong, and, as he would receive the reward of his good deeds, would receive also the punishment of evil deeds. Man did not heed this warning of God, and acquired a knowledge of good and evil, by reason of which we are now responsible for our actions, are involved in evil deeds, and receive the reward of our good deeds. Thus it may be said that this is the prime cause of the coming of evil to man.'—Pt. ii. p. 158.

'Christian divines have made it a basis of their faith that, by the disobedience of Adam and Eve, sin has passed upon all men, and therefore all men are guilty. If their sin was pardoned without any punishment, that would be opposed to justice, and if every one had to bear all his own punishment, that would be opposed to mercy. Therefore God gave the promise of a coming Saviour, namely, Jesus Christ, who is God Himself, but who became incarnate in the form of Christ, who was the seed of the woman, not of the man. . . . But we Mahommedans do not consider this disobedience of Adam and Eve to have been the beginning of sin, nor do we look on this event as bringing guilt on the human race. We believe this event to have been the cause of the knowledge of good and evil for mankind, by reason of which they have not remained void of responsibility like other creatures. If, therefore, any one will walk according to the guidance of God, he shall obtain salvation ; and if any one will act in a way opposed to it, he shall be punished.'—Part ii. pp. 182, 183.

E.

NATURAL RELIGION IN HINDU LITERATURE.

Besides one or two extracts that have already been given, I subjoin the following specimens of high moral and religious sentiments taken from Hindu poets.

The following, found in the Hitopadesa, is translated by Edwin Arnold :—

'*Take no thought for your life*' (Matt. vi. 23-30).

For thy bread be not o'er thoughtful, God for all hath taken thought ;
When the babe is born, the milk too to the mother's breast is brought :
He who gave the swan his silver, and the hawk his plumes of pride,
And his purple to the peacock—He will verily provide.

The following is a translation of a Tamil hymn by Mr. Cardwell :—

'*All Thy works praise Thee*' (compare Ps. cxlvii.)

Whilst Thee, with tongues of splendour, the orbs of heaven praise;
Whilst gems to Thee their voices, with tongues of brilliance, raise;
Whilst unto Thee wood-warblers, with tongues of joyance, sing;
Whilst wood-flowers Thy sweet praises from tongues of fragrance fling;
Whilst Thee, with tongues of clearness, the water-floods applaud:
Thus, day by day, from all things dost Thou receive not laud?
Wilt Thou not deign to suffer the tongue Thou gavest me—
Though I be dumb and thoughtless—to offer praise to Thee?

The following are translated from various Indian writers by Dr. John Muir :—

'*Why beholdest thou the mote which is in thy brother's eye?*' *&c.*

Thou mark'st the faults of other men,
Although as mustard seeds minute;
Thine own escape thy partial ken,
Though each in size a Bilva fruit.

No second youth for Man (compare Job xiv. 7).

The empty beds of rivers fill again,
Trees, leafless now, renew their vernal bloom,
Returning moons their lustrous phase resume,
But man a second youth expects in vain.

The lapse of Time not practically noticed.

Again the morn returns, again the night;
Again the sun, the moon, ascends the sky;
Our lives still waste away as seasons fly,
But who his final welfare keeps in sight?

Good and Bad seem to be equally favoured here; not so hereafter.

Both good and bad the patient earth sustains,
To cheer them both the sun impartial glows,
On both the balmy wind refreshing blows,
On both at once the god Parjanya rains.

So is it here on earth, but not for ever
Shall good and bad be favoured thus alike;
A stern decree the bad and good shall sever,
And vengeance sure, at last, the wicked strike.

The righteous then in realms of light shall dwell,
Immortal, pure, in undecaying bliss;
The bad for long, long years shall pine in hell,
A place of woe, a dark and deep abyss.

Final Overthrow of the Wicked (compare Ps. xxxvii.)

Not even here on earth are blest
Unrighteous men, who thrive by wrong
And guileful arts; who, bold and strong,
With cruel spite the weak molest.

Though goodness only bring distress,
Let none that hallowed path forsake,
Mark what reverses overtake
The wicked after brief success.

Not all at once the earth her fruits
Produces; so unrighteousness
But slowly works, yet not the less
At length the sinner quite uproots.

At first through wrong he grows in strength,
He sees good days, and overthrows,
In strife triumphant, all his foes;
But justice strikes him down at length.

Yes, retribution comes, though slow,
For, if the man himself go free,
His sons shall then the victims be,
Or else his grandsons feel the blow.